Advance Praise for
My China in Tang Poetry

"Susan Wan Dolling has lived with Tang poetry for decades, and like the best teachers she knows how to make her familiarity ours. She tells the stories behind the poems, and her translations, clear and natural and fluid, have a sure sense of how emotions build and shine. Far more than an anthology, this series is a comprehensive tour of Tang poetry and culture with a genial, expert and witty guide."
— James Richardson Poet, Professor of Creative Writing, Emeritus, Lewis Center for the Arts, Princeton University

"This book makes me want to drop everything and do nothing but learn about Chinese poetry! Dolling brings poets Li Bai and Du Fu vividly to life, both in her translations and in the stories she tells about 8th-century China, along with her own memories about growing up in Hong Kong. The notes to the poems cover poetics, wordplay, proverbs, history, geography, legends, folk songs, festivals, food, flowers, and more—everything you need to fall in love with these poems, these poets, and their world."
— Laura Gibbs, author of *Aesop's Fables: A New Translation*, Penguin Classics

"Susan Wan Dolling's fresh translations of Tang poetry is a virtuoso performance...with vivid context and engaging personal anecdotes, Dolling's work interprets the Tang dynasty and its literary luminaries for a new generation of readers."
— Kevin Peraino author of *A Force So Swift: Mao, Truman, and the Birth of Modern China, 1949*, Crown Publishing

"Susan Wan Dolling has given readers, from academics to lovers of poetry, a refreshing and innovative staging of Tang poetry. Informed personal readings accompanied by stories behind the poets and poems capture the enduring appeal of Tang poetry. In my many years of teaching Classical Chinese poetry, this series is a fresh take that is accessible to the general audience unfamiliar with Chinese as well as being delightful for the audience steeped in the tradition (and everyone in between)."

—Chiu-Mi Lai, Ph.D., Professor of Instruction, University of Texas at Austin

"Susan Wan Dolling's My China in Tang Poetry is surprisingly easy and entertaining reading. Susan's scholarship as well as vivid imagination shine through her storytelling and educated postulations, informative for both Tang poetry aficionados and neophytes. Her resplendent translations of the Chinese poetry are brilliant."

—Diana Lin, Hong Kong Journalist

"These volumes are a must for anyone who is interested in the Tang poetry which is the heart of the literature and culture of China."
—Margaret Sun, author of *Betwixt and Between,* Earnshaw Books

"Susan Wan Dolling is a scholar/poet who has breathed and danced these poems every day of her life. These beautiful translations are proof positive that translation is never a matter of just translating words. Thank you, Susan, for this gift of poetry."

—Nadia Benabid, translator of *Return to Painting* by Nobel Laureate Gao Xingjian

"In China, past and present, most kids grow up reciting Tang poems, and some even try their hand at writing these five or seven character lines when they feel inspired. Writing in the genre, usually poems of four or eight lines, might sound simple, but in fact it is not. As one grows older and read more and more of the annotated texts, one becomes more and more appreciative of the details of both the artistry and historical richness of these poems. As translator and annotator of these Tang poems, Susan Wan Dolling has done a fantastic job. The meticulousness of her annotations should be appreciated, and her renderings, accurate and smoothly readable (both script-wise and sound-wise) are definitely enjoyable."

—Diana Yue, Honorary Associate Professor, Hong Kong University, translator of *Flying Carpet: A Tale of Fertillia* by Hong Kong's own Xixi

"Best book ever!"

—Li Bai, poet and drunkard

SUPERSTARS

MY CHINA IN TANG POETRY
VOLUME I

Susan Wan Dolling

Superstars
My China in Tang Poetry Volume I

By Susan Wan Dolling

ISBN-13: 978-988-8843-71-8

© 2024 Susan Wan Dolling

Photographer: Clare Dyer

POETRY / TRANSLATION

EB211

All rights reserved. No part of this book may be reproduced in material form, by any means, whether graphic, electronic, mechanical or other, including photocopying or information storage, in whole or in part. May not be used to prepare other publications without written permission from the publisher except in the case of brief quotations embodied in critical articles or reviews. For information contact info@earnshawbooks.com

Published in Hong Kong by Earnshaw Books Ltd.

For my families in Hong Kong, China,
England, Canada, and the U.S.A.

Contents

Prologue — 1
Superstars: **Li Bai** 李白 **and Du Fu** 杜甫
Basic Information — 3
Preamble — 4

Chapter One　　From Frontier to Palace　　7
Chapter Two　　The Fairest of Them All　　37
Chapter Three　From Palace to Wilderness (Part I)　　55
Chapter Four　　Drinking Songs　　73
Chapter Five　　From Palace to Wilderness (Part II)　　81
Chapter Six　　The Big Picture　　109
Chapter Seven　Country Broken, Land Remains　　129
Chapter Eight　Easy Living in Hard Times　　143
Chapter Nine　　Old Friends on First Meeting　　170
Chapter Ten　　Last Poems　　181

Endnote: Verse Forms — 185
Poets and Dates — 188
Acknowledgements — 189
Epilogue — 192

Prologue

Growing up in Hong Kong, I did not do well in Chinese classes, and often received "big eggs", meaning zeroes, for Chinese "dictation". In this context, dictation means memorizing assigned texts at home, usually from classical Chinese poetry, and then writing them out in class. In addition, such "dictations" had to be done with Chinese ink brushes, not an easy task for little hands to accomplish. Being neither studious nor particularly good at rote learning, I have no fond memories of such endeavors. On the other hand, I was fortunate to have a mother who loved the Chinese classics and would "sing" or "chant" poems and tell stories from them to me, and I absorbed by osmosis. It was not until I left the British colony for college that I discovered Chinese classical poetry for myself. Or you might say, when what I absorbed was given space to blossom.

As I went backwards from studying English Literature, in college and afterwards, to rediscovering Chinese poetry for writing verse under the rubric of "translation workshops" initiated by the American poet, John Peck, at Princeton's Creative Writing Program, I began to "dig" with my "squat pen", to borrow Seamus Heaney's metaphor in "Digging". In those workshops, my mother's voice from faraway sang, as in a duet, in harmony with that of the fiery speech teacher at Diocesan Girls' School which I attended as a kindergartener. This teacher's name was Mrs. O'Connell, and she was the first who taught me how to breathe and dance to the rhythms of English poetry, in what used to be called "Verse-Speaking".

My China in Tang Poetry is the culmination of all this digging,

SUPERSTARS

driven not only by my own love of the stories and poems coming from these roots, but also by my desire to make what I know and love accessible to others who have no Chinese, at least, no classical Chinese and therefore have no way into that world, much of which is still alive and kicking in today's China.

Basic Information

Some background information may be useful for those unfamiliar with the Chinese language in English. The dominant system for Romanizing Chinese used to be the Wade-Giles system, created by two 19th Century British sinologists. After the communist victory in 1949, a new system of Romanization of the spoken word was created, called *Pinyin*, which simply means "phonetics" in Chinese. The government of the People's Republic under Mao Zedong also created a simplified form of the written Chinese language, largely to make Chinese characters easier to learn and therefore promote universal education. In feudal society, the written language belonged only to the privileged. For the sake of simplicity, I mainly use Pinyin in these books. Exceptions are noted. For Chinese characters, I use the traditional or standard script (繁體/正體) because a systematized simplified script (簡體) simply did not exist in Tang China!

A quick word on names that come up so often in these stories. In feudal China, a person's birth name 名 *ming*, is used only by elders and the emperor. Friends and peers or someone in a younger generation calls one by one's courtesy name 字 *zi*. Then there is the pen name 別號 *bie hao*, which can be used to refer to oneself or used by others among the literati. To simplify matters, I simply call them by the name (or names) by which we know them best in literature.

Preamble

On March 21, 2015, the UN issued six stamps to commemorate World Poetry Day. Li Bai's poem, "Quiet Night Thoughts" 静夜思 was one of them.

The poem in Chinese:

靜夜思

牀前明月光，
疑是地上霜。
舉頭望明月，
低頭思故鄉。

My translation:

QUIET NIGHT THOUGHTS

Before my bed, a patch of brilliant moon,
so bright, I took it for frost on the ground.
Looking up, I gaze at that brilliant moon.
Home fills my thoughts as I look down.

Perhaps prompted by this global recognition of his poetry, a conference by the title of "Li Bai and the Silk Road" was held in Kyrgyzstan on October 18 that same year. As reported by China's Xinhua News, one of the main topics discussed is whether this superstar Tang poet is Chinese, Kyrgyzstani or of a mixed race. This was one thousand three hundred and thirteen years after his birth, and in the interim, much ink has been spilt on his ancestry. One hopes the interest in his "birth certificate" (of which there is none) did not have to do with his race, or spring from the need to lay claim to or prove that his blood is "pure". His poetry matters precisely because it opens our minds and our understanding of others and ourselves, and in that, it belongs to everybody, everywhere. Besides, it is his poetry, and not his blood, that makes him Chinese. In this volume, Li Bai aka Li Po, is our first superstar, and "Quiet Night Thoughts" is a poem every school child in China knows.

Our second superstar is Du Fu who was eleven years Li Bai's junior. He would never have guessed, except for a brief moment in his youth when he boasted or hoped that one day, he would stand on top of the highest peaks in China and look down on all the little mountains below, that he would be recognized as such. Du Fu's much-loved poem, "Spring View," was written when Chang'an, the capital, was under siege:

The poem in Chinese:

春望

國破山河在，城春草木深。
感時花濺淚，恨別鳥驚心。
烽火連三月，家書抵萬金。
白頭搔更短，渾欲不勝簪。

My Translation:

SPRING VIEW

Our country is broken, the land remains.
City in spring locked in depths of green.
Tears fall with petals in a gust of wind.
Lingering birds call, startling the heart.

SUPERSTARS

> Three months running, war fires burned.
> I will give anything for word from home.
> This crop of white, thinned from plucking,
> will soon be unable to hold a pin in place.

I shall have more to say about this poem when we get to the Du Fu chapters. Now, let me tell you their stories and put these poems in context.

1
Li Bai 李白
From Frontier to Palace

In the spring of 701, a superstar was born in a place called Suyab, outside of China, in today's Kyrgyzstan. Suyab was in the borderland of the Tang Empire on one of the trade routes that would one day be collectively dubbed the "Silk Road". He was the twelfth child of Li Ke 李客 and Yue Wa 月娃: *Ke* means "guest", *Yue* means "moon" and *Wa* means "doll" or "baby girl". Li Ke was a merchant. Yue Wa is reputed to have been a very beautiful woman and sister to four brave warriors. And, as the story goes, it was through her brothers that she met her future husband.

The night Li Bai was born his mother said she dreamed that the "Great White Star" 太白星 *Tai Bai Xing*, that is, Venus, fell from the sky. Thus, they named him Li Bai, with the courtesy name of *Taibai*. When the new Tang Emperor, Xuanzong ascended the throne in 712, Li Bai was almost eleven. By then the family had moved to Chengdu in China and registered as Sichuan residents. Li Bai was four or five when they arrived there and, for the rest of his life, identified himself as a native of Sichuan, or a part of Shu 蜀 as it was then called.

Some have suggested that Li Ke moved the whole family into China proper for the specific purpose of grooming this child to become a scholar-official for the Tang court. Had the family not been traders, this would not have been such an outrageous idea, as becoming a scholar-official was the way to climb the social ladder in feudal Chinese society. Being in the merchant-trader class, however, the family was socially just above slaves. The following is what the social hierarchy in Tang China looked like:

Emperor and His Family
Aristocrats
Scholar-Officials and Bureaucrats
Eunuchs
Imperial Family Servants
Buddhist and Daoist Clergy
Peasants
Artisans and Merchants
Slaves

There were laws governing what each group might or might not own or wear, down to the color of their clothes and furnishings. For example, only aristocrats were allowed to wear silk and only scholar-officials and above were allowed red doors.

Li Ke was quite successful as a merchant, but it is not entirely clear whether he was "pure" Han Chinese, Han being the majority ethnic group in the Chinese empire by far and therefore the most powerful or "legitimate". In any case, we know for sure the woman he married was not Chinese. Ha Jin, in his concise and suggestive introduction to Li Bai's origins, suggests she was a Turk. Ha, among others, also surmised the Li family had committed some serious offense in a previous generation and was therefore banished from China, so when Li Ke moved his family to Shu, which was inside Chinese territory, he might have been doing so illegally. Li Ke, on the other hand, claimed to be a fifth-generation descendant of the great general Li Guang 李廣 (184-119 BCE) and therefore distantly related to the Tang dynasty's royal family who also claimed Li Guang as ancestor. It was perhaps because of this fact or fantasy that Li Ke dared dream his talented little boy Li Bai could very well be the family's chance to reclaim their Chinese identity and climb back onto the Tang social ladder. (Ha Jin, *The Banished Immortal: A Life of Li Bai*, New York: Pantheon Books, 2019).

The Imperial Examination system had its beginnings in Han dynasty China four or five hundred years previously, but it was not until the Tang dynasty that it became consistently used to discover new talents. Moreover, unless you were already in a scholar-official family – during Li Bai's time at least, though later this rule became somewhat relaxed – you were not allowed to take the exam, except in special circumstances, for example if someone with status recommended you. In other words, Li Ke's fond hope for his brilliant son was, from the beginning, a pipe dream. Having this back story about his childhood offers us some insight into Li Bai's poetry and his purposefully mysterious beginnings. Moreover, some Li Bai readers prefer his life to be shrouded in mystery and romance, and he himself seemed to have enjoyed the bad boy-genius image and embraced the idea that he was dropped from heaven, often repeating the nickname He Zhizhang was to give him as a "banished immortal".

There is little or no mention of Suyab anywhere in his writing. Even his father and siblings were rarely mentioned, let alone his mother and her side of the family. What little there is of such familial information, we gather from his contemporaries and from the two *Books of Tang, Old and New*, compiled in 941-945. It was not until after he left home that Li Bai started talking about himself and his relationships with others in his writings, and even then, it was mostly friends he mentioned. It is hard to tell if a great deal of what he said about his ancestry is part of that "self-creation" Ha Jin reminds us of in *The Banished Immortal*.

Li Bai was no shrinking violet though and was not shy about telling us that by age ten, he had read all the classics, such as histories of the Spring and Autumn Warring States Period and the writings of Kongzi (hereafter referred to as Confucius), Zhuangzi, and other philosophers, and he was already reading esoteric texts and making poetry. His father was his main teacher when he was little. The father must have felt like those parents who suddenly realize they have a prodigy on their hands, and that the child is quickly surpassing them in knowledge and ability. Li Ke began looking for help with his son's education, first around where they lived, and then, farther and farther away. Li Bai, at puberty, was not only an accomplished scholar and poet, but skilled in swordsmanship and calligraphy. He could also play some musical instruments such as the qin and the flute. Some of this he learned from Buddhist and Daoist masters that he sought out near where he lived, and from whom he also learned how to tame wild birds. One imagines this latter skill entails sitting very still in meditation until the birds chose to land on him.

Since he was not allowed to take the Imperial Exams because of his social status, he needed someone well-connected to recommend him, and Li Ke was eager to show off his son. In 720, Li Bai was interviewed by Su Ting, an aged governor and highly respected member of the literati. Su thought the young man had superior talent and said he should become a scholar-official, but it was all talk. Li Bai was nineteen at the time. This was in Chengdu, where our poet first attempted to make connections, but he met with little success. Instead, he made a name for himself as an amusing and brilliant poet, a good drinker and a good friend to many who needed financial assistance, but somewhat of an arrogant so-and-so to others. After five years, his brush and his sword, and no doubt his tongue, had all gotten him in trouble in one way or another. He finally decided it was time to leave Sichuan and look for better opportunities in more prosperous parts of the country.

His father had money and supported his efforts. The logical thing to do would be to head straight for Chang'an, the capital. Instead, the wealthy tradesman's son headed for the coast, like a tourist. This was 724 and he was twenty-three years old. He sailed down the Yangtze to Dongting Lake, then towards today's Nanjing. As a student of Daoism, Li Bai was in the habit of looking for immortals or at least wise men or hermits, and these were most likely to live in mountains. Thus, he stopped by Emei Shan 峨嵋山, a sacred Sichuan Mountain, one of four sacred to the Buddhists, before leaving Shu. This is a range with three peaks and is so named because they are as shapely as the moth's brow. As to why a moth's brow is considered beautiful you shall have to wait until we get to the "Moth Brow Mountain Moon Song".

The moon appears often in Chinese poetry, and often in poems of longing. The lunar calendar, which is the traditional Chinese calendar, is full of references to the moon, and significantly, there are two especially important festivals that celebrate the moon, one is the First Full Moon of the New Year, and the other is the Mid-Autumn Festival celebrating the Harvest Moon. Both are occasions for family gatherings. Thus, the moon often reminds one of family or home, and as the moon is round, the family gathers around a round table for the feast celebrating the festival. We say metaphorically, when a family member is missing, "the moon is round, [too bad] the family is not whole [i.e., someone is missing]". In other words, the moon pervades Chinese culture. Even so, Li Bai readers will agree the moon appears obsessively in his poetry, especially in the early poems. The moon is a good companion, especially to drinkers, and especially when one is drinking alone. It is worth mentioning, however, that the word "moon" appears in the names of both his mother (Moon Child/Doll) and his sister (Round Moon), and later, in his son's nickname. In his early poems, it seems to me, his mother was never far from his thoughts, even though she was unmentionable, because it would call attention to his own "foreignness". Calling on the moon was to call his mother by her name. If I am right, then the "you" in the following poem is meant for that beautiful woman who loved and nurtured him in the early years of his life.

The following poem was written in a seven-character *jueju*. It might be called one of his many travel poems. It is also one of the first where he perfected the trick of using actual place names in the lines of the poem without disrupting the flow of the verse. This makes it difficult to translate. The poem is called *E Mei Shan Yue Ge*, which I have translated as "Moth Brow Mountain Moon Song". [*E* is pronounced like the *uh* part of *huh*?] As noted above, *Emei Shan* 峨嵋山 is the name of a sacred Buddhist Mountain, where *emei* means moth brow and *shan* means mountain. It is situated in the area just outside of where Li Bai grew up. In this poem, we are at the beginning of his journey out of Shu.

Now, a beautiful woman's brow is also described as *e mei* 蛾眉, and when the two characters are used to indicate the beautiful woman herself, they are written with a woman radical 娥媚 and pronounced the same way. Moreover, there are three ways to write the word *e*, which are all related to one another. The difference among them lies in the radical: when the word describes the name of a mountain, as in this case, we use the mountain radical 山; when it describes the moth, we use the worm radical 虫; and when it describes a woman, we use the woman radical 女. The origin of all three words is the moth's antennae, which are thought to look like a pair of brows: a pair of beautiful eyebrows on a woman is called *e mei*, "moth brows," and by extension, a beautiful woman is also called *e mei*, with the woman radical. In Hong Kong, there is a small beach or cove, popular with snorkelers, mostly people with private yachts, called *Emei Wan* (also called Crescent Cove in English, which interestingly, takes us back to the image of the moon), where the *e* in its name is written with the woman radical. In other words, the meaning of "*emei*" all goes back to the moth and its beautiful antennae. Thus, I feel quite justified in translating Emei Shan as Moth Brow Mountain.

In "Moth Brow Mountain Moon Song," Li Bai uses five place names in four lines and has them flow right into the prosody. I have translated "Moth Brow Mountain" in the title, substituted "Blue Coat Waters", another name for "Pingjiang" in the original second line; translated "Clear Brook," dropped the "Three Gorges," from the original third line; and substituted "home" for "Yuzhou" that was in the Chinese fourth line. Yuzhou is in the last line in the Chinese and is today's Chongxing or Chungking in Sichuan or Shu. "Three Gorges" is named in the third line, but it is unclear whether by "Three Gorges" Li Bai meant the "little three gorges" nearby or the well-known "Three Gorges", which are farther away, but both are in the direction of Yuzhou, the direction he was going toward, but with his back to it. I have had to drop "Yuzhou" and insert "home" in the English line (which is in the opposite direction), to capture the fact that he was looking toward home while sailing away from it. Thus, I was only able to save three out of five place names in the translation.

SUPERSTARS

MOTH BROW MOUNTAIN MOON SONG

Half a wheel of the autumn moon peers over Moth Brow Mountain,
diving its reflection into the Blue Coat Waters, bobbing on the waves.
We left Clear Brook before morning broke, facing home, sailing away.
I think of you but cannot see you, leaving you farther and farther behind.

峨眉山月歌

峨眉山月半輪秋，
影入平羌江水流。
夜發清溪向三峽，
思君不見下渝州。

Further along this journey, he reaches The Gate of Thorns, or Jingmen 荊門, which was about midway between his home near Chengdu in Shu and Shan Zhong, his destination near the coast, as he traveled along the Yangtze. He was basically sailing along the Yangtze or Chang Jiang 長江 which I mostly translate as The Great River when I do not call it the Yangtze. "The ancient Kingdom of Chu" in the second line, is a strong and important state during the Spring and Autumn Period, which included most of present-day Hubei and Hunan.

MY CHINA IN TANG POETRY

PASSING THROUGH GATE OF THORNS

I have sailed through faraway Gate of Thorns,
arriving to visit the ancient Kingdom of Chu.
Mountains have plateaued into wide open plains
and the river enters a vast wilderness of nothing.
The moon throws her sky mirror on the dark water
where bulging clouds have built a mirage of palaces.
The river has come with me these ten thousand miles
from my hometown, to see me off on this long journey.

渡荊門送別

渡遠荊門外，來從楚國遊。
山隨平野盡，江入大荒流。
月下飛天鏡，雲生結海樓。
仍憐故鄉水，萬里送行舟。

Shan Zhong 剡中 is the ancient name for the area near present day Nanjing. The Kingdom of Chu mentioned above also wraps round Shan Zhong. As we shall see, it was significant to Li Bai for many reasons, and he would be returning here more than once. The first reason for Shan Zhong's importance to Li Bai is because this was Xie Lingyun country. Xie Lingyun 謝靈運 (365-433) was the first poet to make landscape the focus of a poem. This genre of poetry came to be called "mountain and river poetry", 山水詩. His famous long poem, "Shan Ju Fu" or "Living in the Mountains, a *Fu*", was based on the landscape of Shan Zhong. The fact that he was a traveler, a mountain lover, and a poet, in addition to being the grandson of a general, naturally made him attractive to Li Bai. He appeared often in the latter's poetry.

The second reason for Shan Zhong's attraction was that, even before Xie's time, this was the area where the State of Yue 越, and the State of Wu 吳, were situated. These were states during the end of the Spring and Autumn Era when there were many states. Among them, there were two kings, the King of Wu, Fuchai 夫差 (495-473 BCE) and the King of Yue, Goujian 勾踐 (496-465 BCE) whose stories had captured Li Bai's imagination very early on. Again, we shall be meeting them often and their stories will be told soon.

And thirdly, it is beautiful country, and in the mountains, its beauty is unearthly. Since he was in search of immortals all his life, this area was surely one obvious place to look. Li Bai was torn between the two extremes of seeking worldly success and serving his country on the one hand and, on the other, leaving it all behind and searching for Daoist immortality instead.

Finally, the expression, "arriving with sail intact", is an allusion to an ancient Han text meaning, "I arrived safely." Chinese people are always going places with the sole aim of tasting some dish or other. Shan Zhong is apparently famous for its minced sea-perch.

LEAVING GATE OF THORNS IN THE FALL

> Frost fills the Gate of Thorns, trees all bare,
> my boat and I have arrived with sail intact.
> This trip was not for their minced sea-perch,
> I am heading for Shan Zhong's mountains.

秋下荊門

霜落荊門江樹空，
布帆無恙掛秋風。
此行不為鱸魚鱠，
自愛名山入剡中。

MY CHINA IN TANG POETRY

Li Bai wrote quite a few "frontier poems", either imagining himself to be at the frontier, from whence he sprang, or as the person/woman/wife elsewhere in China who is missing a soldier at the frontier. The following three are favorites. They have all been much anthologized. Dates are uncertain. In "Frontier Moon", "Sky Mountain" is *Tian Shan* 天山, a mountain range that runs partly in China and partly in Kyrgyzstan. Gate of Jade, *Yumen*, 玉門, is a frontier post on the trade route. It is an important pass between China and the Western Region. The Battle of *Baideng*, 百登之戰 in 200 BCE, is famous enough that I have kept its Chinese name in the poem. "Tartar country" is loosely used by the Chinese to refer to all foreigners to the north and west. Emperor Gaozu of the Han dynasty and its founder (202 BCE) invaded them, hoping to subjugate them, but failed, and ended up negotiating a treaty whereby Han China paid annual tributes to the tribe and sent princesses as peace offerings in marriage to the Tartar tribal lords. This practice kept peace for sixty years till Han Wu Di, 漢武帝 (sometimes translated as the Warrior King of Han) decided to send commoners instead of princesses to the "barbarians". They thought the "barbarians" would not be able to tell the difference. Fighting resumed.

SUPERSTARS

FRONTIER MOON

The bright moon rises from Sky Mountain,
peering over an ocean of billowing clouds.
This wind has come a long, long way,
blowing hard through the Gate of Jade.
Baideng Pass is still filled with Han soldiers:
across Clear Blue Lake, Tartars keep watch.
This has ever been the battleground between
the two forces, and no one has ever returned.
A frontier guard gazes back from the border,
his long face speaks of bitter longing for home.
At home, someone is waiting on a high tower,
sighing at the same moon in helpless despair.

關山月

明月出天山，蒼茫雲海間。
長風幾萬里，吹度玉門關。
漢下白登道，胡窺青海灣。
由來征戰地，不見有人還。
戍客望邊邑，思歸多苦顏。
高樓當此夜，嘆息未應閒。

One could say he was sympathizing with the soldiers and their loved ones, or one could say the poet was borrowing their voices. Sky Mountain range is partly in China and partly in Kyrgyzstan which reminds one of Li Bai's birthplace. Plus, the Gate of Jade itself must be the gate where his family came through when they moved to Jiangyou in Sichuan from Suyab. In the next poem, the moon is out again. Butterflies almost always mean lovers, as ghosts or as living beings. Again, the above speculations apply.

MY CHINA IN TANG POETRY

THINKING OF YOU AT THE FRONTIER

What time was it last year, my husband, when you left me?
In our south garden above the green grass, butterflies hover.
What time of year is it? How long since have I missed you?
On West Mountain, snow piles high behind clouds of Qin.
Three thousand miles you have travelled to the Gate of Jade,
your voice, letters, news of you, not a word has reached me.

思邊

去年何時君別妾，南園綠草飛蝴蝶。
今歲何時妾憶君，西山白雪暗晴雲。
玉關去此三千里，欲寄音書那可聞？

SPRING THOUGHTS

Grass on Swallow Bank like emerald silk,
old mulberries bend low their heavy heads.
On the day you dream of coming home,
that day is when longing breaks my heart.
This spring wind doesn't even know me,
what's it doing behind my bed curtains?

春思

燕草如碧絲，秦桑低綠枝。
當君懷歸日，是妾斷腸時。
春風不相識，何事入羅幃？

SUPERSTARS

It is hard to tell with some of Li Bai's "love poems" that sound so personal, if he was borrowing voices to speak of his own longing, or if he was lending his voice to others, as he was such an empathetic listener that some people have asked him to write for them, or whether he was simply imagining such scenarios. In any case, readers are free to insert themselves into the "I" of these poems.

It is often said of Chinese classical poetry that there is no "I", because grammatically, we don't often see the word "I" used. Those who believe this have made a whole world view out of it. For my part, I don't think this is true, particularly with the lyrics. More likely, the "I" is assumed, the poet is accepted as the speaker, or readers are invited to place themselves into the poem if they so desire.

At this point in the story, you may be wanting a map to show you where Li Bai was and where he went, generally though, in these early years, he was simply traveling down the Yangtze towards the coast. Traveling on rivers was the easiest way to go from A to B, especially if one were going on long trips.

Li Bai's most famous moon poem is the one every Chinese child learns when they first meet the poet at home or at school. "Quiet Night Thoughts," which I introduced in the Preamble, was written as a five-character *jueju*. At the same time, there is another poem written as a *pailu* that expresses similar sentiments but in this freer and longer form. (See Endnotes for "Verse Forms.") In fact, they could very well have been written on the same night. I imagine Li Bai reciting "Quiet Night Thoughts" out by the well, coming into his room, trying to fall asleep, maybe sleeping a little, but soon getting up, feeling he had more to say, sitting down, reaching for his ink brush, and finishing his thoughts in the longer poem. I thought it would be a fun exercise to place them together here to compare the two. Before going to the longer poem, let us take another look at "Quiet Night Thoughts".

Simple poems are often the hardest to render into another language. When a poem has imbedded itself into the cultural imagination, as this poem has done, the demand on the translator is even greater. I have often, over the years, wondered what gives this simple poem its power. Beyond the moon and homesickness, there is something else at work. In a moment of epiphany while obsessing over this, I came upon my answer. It is the flood of moonlight, emptying the mind of the very purpose of his travels, his talents and his ambition and the myriad responsibilities and secrets they carry, washed away, in that single moment, when the moon came flooding into his mind, bringing in thoughts of the home he left behind. Thus, I offer you a slightly different rendition of this poem below.

QUIET NIGHT THOUGHTS

Before my bed, a patch of brilliant moon,
so bright, I took it for frost on the ground.
Looking up, I gaze at that brilliant moon.
Home floods my mind as I look down.

靜夜思

牀前明月光,
疑是地上霜。
舉頭望明月,
低頭思故鄉。

SUPERSTARS

I have kept the translation of the first word 牀 *chuang* as "bed" in both my translations even though some commentators have claimed the word probably referred to the frame of a well, and the brightness of the moon indicates that Li Bai was more likely outdoors standing next to a well than he would be indoors beside a bed. The reason for my recalcitrance is that the word has been understood by so many children and adults for so long as "bed," that there is a certain cultural nostalgia associated with the reading of "bed" instead of "well" here, and I do not wish to deprive the bilingual reader of that familiarity. Thus, let me apologize for our collective clinging onto this mistake. That said, there is also the ancient idiom, 飲水思源, *yin shui si yuan*, which means "when you drink water you should remember its origin," in other words, "do not forget where you came from." And this, when we read his other poems, could indeed make the well even more significant, even if the source of water is not necessarily a well but a river or a spring.

Now, for the longer poem:

A TRAVELER'S THOUGHTS ON AN AUTUMN EVENING

> A chilly breeze crosses the autumn sea,
> blowing my thoughts towards the old homestead,
> over countless mountain ridges, flying
> against the river's flow. Can rivers flow upstream?
> Cloud colors dim at the far end of the sky.
> Bright moonlight breaks this traveler's heart.
> Grass is no longer green or tender, fragrance gone.
> Icy dewdrops tell us it's time for winter clothes.

MY CHINA IN TANG POETRY

The Silver River sinks deep into dreams,[1]
and the stars have all faded when I awake
and taste of the old country fills my senses.
Who can shoo away tears when they come?

秋夕旅懷

涼風度秋海，吹我鄉思飛。
連山去無際，流水何時歸。
目極浮雲色，心斷明月暉。
芳草歇柔艷，白露催寒衣。
夢長銀漢落，覺罷天星稀。
含悲想舊國，泣下誰能揮。

During this time of traveling, making new friends, and establishing contacts who might recommend him for officialdom, Li Bai also met many others from all walks of life, including singing girls and/or prostitutes. He patronized wine shops, taverns, tea houses, and other houses of pleasure, and was told as many stories as he told others. He had the knack of producing verses extemporaneously which people found very entertaining. Word spread. And he drank a lot, sometimes being paid for his poetry in drinks. Plus, he still had his father's money. This was a young man traveling alone, coming from the provinces into prosperous cities. He had much entertainment to offer and many new experiences to be had.

An aside: there are quite a few poems about young girls whose charms men find irresistible, and I do have reservations about translating them, because the girls were so young, and in many cases, they were "entertainers". I have no intention of

---

[1] Silver River is what the Chinese call the Milky Way. I have used both terms interchangeably in my various translations.

encouraging the objectification of the "exotic Oriental" woman. Nonetheless, I find the best of these poems vivid and tender, and I remind myself that people died much younger, and they had to take on adult responsibilities much sooner. Fifteen and even younger was the marriageable age at the time. Moreover, many of these scholar-poet-wanderers like Li Bai compared themselves to these young women, forever on the asking or pleading end, trying to please, waiting for a morsel, forever looking in from the outside, on the fringes of society looking into where they want to be in society. There is a famous couplet in Bai Juyi's "Pipa Song" that runs: "Castaways, we drift together and part again, / I know you well without knowing you at all," that expresses this sentiment very well. In other words, they were not objectifying these women (at least not in the poems I choose to translate) but thought of them as friends, adrift in society, like themselves.

The following poem, "Drink with Me," though, is not terribly profound. It is just a playful, flirty poem, and not often anthologized. It begins with two exotic images: grape wine and golden cups. Chinese wine was made mostly with rice and drunk in clay cups or bowls. Grape wine is foreign, from the west, maybe Persia, and gold cups suggest decadence. Li Bai apparently loved red wine. The "lispy twang" describes a speech characteristic of the Wu region, and the hibiscus curtain in the last line refers to the bed curtain. The rest is self-explanatory. Later we will see another poem by the same title that the older Li Bai wrote.

MY CHINA IN TANG POETRY

DRINK WITH ME

> She pours you grape wine
> in golden cups, and she's
> just fifteen, the girl of Wu.
> She comes astride a pony,
> her soft cotton boots so red.
> Brows painted pure black,
> singing with a lispy twang.
> What can you do but concur
> when she leans against you,
> behind the hibiscus curtain?

對酒

葡萄酒，金叵羅，吳姬十五細馬馱，
青黛畫眉紅錦靴，道字不正嬌唱歌，
玳瑁筵中盃中醉，芙蓉帳裏奈君何。

He was also intrigued by some of the stories he heard and made those into poems and became well-known for doing this even in those early years of travel. The following, "Ballad of Long Pole" (I) and (II) are two of these; they are so popular that a couple of idioms have emerged from them into common usage: "green plums and bamboo horse," 青梅竹馬, *qing mei zhu ma,* is an expression used to describe husband and wife who grew up together from a very young age, and 兩少無猜, *liang shao wu cai,* "[growing] up side by side, without deceit or suspicion" is used to describe happy young couples or even two happy children playing together. Ezra Pound's translation of the first of the two Long Pole ballads as "The River Merchant's Wife" from Ernst Fenollosa's Japanese crib of the poem has made it familiar to

SUPERSTARS

English poetry readers. At the time of his translation, Pound had little knowledge of the Chinese language. Nonetheless, this remains one of his most successful translations from the Chinese, with just a few inaccuracies and near misses.

Here are a few pre-reading notes to help you understand the poem: First, 長干, *Chang Gan,* is the name of the fishing village which I translated as Long Pole, for rowing perhaps. Around the middle of the poem, we find a bridge, a terrace, and some hidden rocks. The bridge is a reference to a story from Zhuangzi, of a man waiting for a woman to come to him at the bridge, when a flood came and he wouldn't leave and was drowned holding onto the pillars, waiting. The terrace in the next line refers to the "husband lookout" nearby. In the original it is husband-lookout-platform or tower. Such spots are not uncommon on mountains or hills, especially those near the coast. The hidden rocks refer to a huge pile of rocks that is submerged in the water there at the Three Gorges in the fifth month during floods and is very dangerous for travelers. That is why he "couldn't be reached" in the next line. Finally, Sanba near the end of the poem is another name for Badong, a place we shall see again.

MY CHINA IN TANG POETRY

BALLAD OF LONG POLE Poem I

When my hair had grown long enough for bangs,
I played theater with branches at our front door.
You came by on your bamboo horse, and we picked
green plums together, throwing them across the well.
We were neighbors at Long Pole Village, grew up
side by side, both strangers to deceit and suspicion.
Then, at fourteen, I was made your wife, my love,
and became so shy after our wedding night. I was
lowering my head, facing the wall, hiding in the dark.
You called and called me before I would turn around.
At fifteen I finally learned to relax my brow,
and swore to be buried in the dust with you.
I thought you would be the one at the bridge,
who knew I would be waiting at the tower?
When I was sixteen, you had to travel far,
to the hidden rocks of the Three Gorges.
In the fifth month, you couldn't be reached,
only the gibbons' howl touched the heavens.
That bald patch you made, walking back and forth,
has grown full of moss at our front door, moss so thick
the broom got stuck, there was no point in sweeping.
Then came autumn winds blowing down all the leaves.
In the eighth month, butterflies appeared again,
flying in pairs over the grass in our west garden.
Seeing them hurt my heart.
Sadness has made me old.
When can I come to Sanba to wait for you?
Send me a letter before you come home,
I don't care how far I must go,
I'll run all the way to Windy Sands.

SUPERSTARS

長干行二首
其一

妾發初覆額，折花門前劇。
郎騎竹馬來，繞床弄青梅。
同居長干裡，兩小無嫌猜，
十四為君婦，羞顏未嘗開。
低頭向暗壁，千喚不一回。
十五始展眉，願同塵與灰。
常存抱柱信，豈上望夫台。
十六君遠行，瞿塘灩澦堆。
五月不可觸，猿聲天上哀。
門前遲行跡，一一生綠苔。
苔深不能掃，落葉秋風早。
八月胡蝶來，雙飛西園草。
感此傷妾心，坐愁紅顏老。
早晚下三巴，預將書報家。
相迎不道遠，直至長風沙。

Here are three things to remember for the next poem: Floating Cloud is the name of a famous swift horse in the Han Dynasty. And Sweet Grass Island is a place name but also one dreams of sweet grass when one is missing one's love. Finally, mandarin ducks signify lovers and kingfishers are also popular birds for sewing on blankets or used for other decorations such as screens and often given as wedding gifts.

MY CHINA IN TANG POETRY

BALLAD OF LONG POLE Poem II

When I was a young girl in my father's house,
I had no idea what smoke and dust could mean.
Then, I was married to my Long Pole man, and
I learned to read the wind, waiting at the beach.
In the fifth month, when the south wind rises,
my husband should be in Baling.
In the eighth month, when the west wind rises,
he must be leaving Yangtze Crossing.
Tears on coming back, tears on leaving,
he's gone more often than he's at home.
I count the days, guess at his arrival at the Lakes,
and my dreams go ashore ahead of the waves.
Last night, a wild storm erupted,
blew down that tall tree by the river.
Darker than the forest the dark storm blew.
What man can walk through that wind?
Only Floating Cloud can forge the way
to keep our date on Sweet Grass Island.
Mandarin ducks waddling on our blanket,
kingfisher birds swimming on the screen.
How I wasted my fifteen years,
cheeks pink as a peach blossom then.
Now I am a merchant's wife, worrying
about the winds, worrying about the waters.

SUPERSTARS

其二

憶妾深閨裡，煙塵不曾識。
嫁與長干人，沙頭候風色。
五月南風興，思君下巴陵。
八月西風起，想君發揚子。
去來悲如何，見少離別多。
湘潭幾日到，妾夢越風波。
昨夜狂風度，吹折江頭樹。
淼淼暗無邊，行人在何處。
好乘浮雲驄，佳期蘭渚東。
鴛鴦綠蒲上，翡翠錦屏中。
自憐十五餘，顏色桃花紅。
那作商人婦，愁水復愁風。

The following is a small sample of the girls and women Li Bai met, some at a distance, some closer, and some intimately, it would seem.

AGGRIEVED

A pretty maid rolls up her blind,
deep in thought, brows tightly knit,
tear stains still wet for all to see.
Wonder who made her so unhappy?

怨情

美人卷珠簾，
深坐顰蛾眉。
但見淚痕濕，
不知心恨誰。

MY CHINA IN TANG POETRY

WAITING FOR YOU TILL LATE

Chilly dewdrops on my jade steps made
my silk socks wet. It's too late to wait outside.
Crystals tinkle as I let down the crystal blind,
I am admiring the moon in her autumn finery.

玉階怨

玉階生白露,
夜久侵羅襪。
卻下水晶簾,
玲瓏望秋月。

Notes for the next poem: North Chamber is where the women folk reside, and a great performance is said to circle the ceiling beams for three days after it ends. An alternate translation of the last line might read: "even if you sing ten thousand songs to make the dust fly on her ceiling beam."

A SERENADE

Long nights, cold nights, sleepless nights in winter:
sitting in sullen silence, sighing in North Chamber,
well water turns to ice as the cold moon enters her room.
The hazy green of her candlelight colors her sad sobbing.
Suddenly, the light goes off,
and her sobs multiply.
His song reaches her,
she rubs her eyes to listen.
The singing in the dark
touches her heart:

SUPERSTARS

voice and feeling
coming together.
Careful, one wrong word and she'll turn on you,
even if your voice circles her ceiling beam for ever after.

夜坐吟

冬夜夜寒覺夜長，
沉吟久坐坐北堂。
冰合井泉月入閨，
金缸青凝照悲啼。
金缸滅，
啼轉多。
掩妾淚，
聽君歌。
歌有聲，
妾有情。
情聲合，
兩無違。
一語不入意，
從君萬曲梁塵飛。

THE MAIDS OF YUE
(one of five poems)

Pretty lotus pickers on the Brook of Ye, singing
as they work, see unfamiliar faces approaching,
turn their boats round, rowing into the lotus fronds,
blushing and giggling, refusing to greet the visitors.

MY CHINA IN TANG POETRY

越女詞五首 其一

耶溪採蓮女，
見客棹歌回。
笑入荷花去，
佯羞不出來。

The next poem has been open to conjecture by some readers as to who Li Bai was writing about or to whom he was writing. It might not even be a personal poem as he might be ghost-writing for someone. On the other hand, he had been in Badong and was possibly on the banks of the Han River. Guessing aside, the nature of the relationship here is obvious.

SENT TO SOMEONE I USED KNOW IN BADONG FROM THE BANKS OF THE HAN RIVER

Agitated waves of Han waters spread far and wide,
cloud and rain flitter and swirl on Witch Mountain.
The east wind comes through my dreams, blowing
westward, landing at your door. I wake to find that
thoughts of White King are still fresh on my mind,
and I'm still wondering why you missed our date.
The merchants from your area often pass through,
don't make me wait too long now to hear from you.

江上寄巴東故人

漢水波浪遠，巫山雲雨飛。
東風吹客夢，西落此中時。
覺後思白帝，佳人與我違。
瞿塘饒賈客，音信莫令稀。

SUPERSTARS

Though many commentators say that this poem was sent to "an old friend", I find that reading a little coy. The poem sounds to me more like one written to a lover whom he had left behind. I make this conjecture particularly because of his use of the expression "cloud and rain", which is a euphemism for intercourse, especially in connection with Witch Mountain (See "A Suite for My Lady" in the next chapter for more on this). He must surely have used this expression deliberately. Badong 巴東 is an old name for Kuizhou 巕州; it is situated along the Yangtze where he had passed through.

These several love poems might give the impression that all Li Bai was doing was having fun spending his father's money, but the more pressing pursuit of seeking out people with connections to recommend him to office was never far from his mind. After three years away from home and having little to show for it, one of his friends, a local official named Meng Rong, advised him to look up a Xu family who lived close by in Anlu. This friend suggested that since the Xus were a well-established family with an unmarried daughter, if Li Bai were to be accepted as suitable, and if he were to marry her, then perhaps this would be another way to get to know more people of consequence. Thus, Li Bai was married for the first time in 727. The patriarch of the Xu family liked his writings and made many introductions for him. Li Bai's new wife was also an educated woman and appreciated his work. Unfortunately, because the Xu family had no son, they had adopted a cousin, who felt threatened by Li Bai, and made life difficult for him. In the end, Li Bai moved out, first to a Xu family property in the mountains and eventually went on the road again.

Then, after these ten years of wandering, or at least of coming and going (725-735), and what must have felt to him like bowing and scraping, to no avail, Li Bai had had enough, at least, for the time being. He called the last ten years "wasted years" of his life. From our perspective, even though many of his thousands of poems are lost to us, these years are hardly wasted, as we are still able to retrieve some of the many poems from this period.

In 729, Li Bai became a father. He did not take very long trips from home for a while and a couple of years later, his second child was born. Now, they have a girl and a boy. After a decade of marriage, his wife died. Between her death and his leaving for Chang'an in 742, he was said to have married another educated woman from a wealthy family who died after a few years and had two other longer-term relationships. One, with a woman named Liu and the other with one named Lu. The first one ended badly with the woman leaving him (this is "the stupid woman" in the next poem) and the second one somewhat better, partly, maybe due to the change in circumstance around his prospects.

The change in circumstance came in 742. Finally, the Emperor sent for him. There were various stories as to who made the recommendation, the Daoist Wu Yun, or another Daoist, He Zhizhang, who was the Palace librarian and became his friend, or was it his lifelong friend, the hermit, Yuan Danqiu who recommended him to Princess Yuzhen. Since some commentators have said that he did not meet He Zhizhang until after his summons by the emperor, it might have more likely been one of the other two friends. No matter, he was on his way up. When the emperor's summons arrived, he was traveling. Thus, the opening line to the next poem.

"The Story of Zhu Maichen" is found in the *Hanshu* (*History of Han*): Zhu Maichen lived in Huiqi and was very poor in his early years. He sold firewood for a living and was a scholar. He could often be seen reading a book even as he took firewood to market. His wife couldn't stand being so poor and left him. Later, Emperor Wu of Han discovered him and made him Prefect of

Huiqi. "That stupid woman" here, borrowed from Zhu's story to refer to Liu, was the woman who lived with Li Bai for a while but had left him, just like Zhu Maichen's wife, and in his case, it was because she thought he was a drunk and a failure. Lastly, Qin is an antiquated way to refer to the capital, Chang'an. Qin 秦 is the dynasty previous to Han 漢, and both are often used as synonym for China.

ON MY WAY TO THE CAPITAL, STOPPING TO SAY GOODBYE TO THE CHILDREN AT NANLING

Home from the mountains to find white wine just fermented and chickens looking fat, picking and pecking at autumn feed. I tell the houseboy to make a meat dish to go with the wine as my little children sing and laugh and pull on my clothes. Singing while drinking is just the thing to do, how true. Let's get up and dance and compete for light with the sinking sun. Many miles I've traveled, so many people I've seen, so late in the day to start this long journey, my horse is raring to go. Tell the stupid woman at Huiqi who looked down on Maichen that I, too, must say goodbye to my family and go west to Qin. Tossing my head back, laughing to the sky as I go out the door. People like us cannot be obscure for long, hidden in wild grass.

南陵別兒童入京

白酒新熟山中歸，黃雞啄黍秋正肥。
呼童烹雞酌白酒，兒女嬉笑牽人衣。
高歌取醉欲自慰，起舞落日爭光輝。
遊說萬乘苦不早，著鞭跨馬涉遠道。
會稽愚婦輕買臣，余亦辭家西入秦。
仰天大笑出門去，我輩豈是蓬蒿人。

2

The Fairest of Them All

Xishi lived sometime near the end of the fifth century BCE. She was so beautiful that when she gazed into a pond of fish, they drowned from losing themselves in her gaze, forgetting how to swim. Then, there was Wang Zhaojun, who was so beautiful and played the pipa so well that wild geese forgot how to fly and fell to their death when she started playing. She lived in the first century BCE. They gave rise to the saying沉鱼落雁, *chen yu luo yan*, "fish drown, geese fall," to describe extremely beautiful women. Xishi and Wang Zhaojun were the first two of the so-called "Four Great Beauties of China". The third beauty was a fictional character. Her name was Diaochan and she lived at the end of the Han dynasty in the second century CE. She was dreamt up by Luo Guanzhong, some say based on a real person, for *Romance of the Three Kingdoms,* a historical novel first published in 1522.

  All three of these beauties saved their people. Xishi was trained to be a spy and used as bait to entice the king of an enemy state. Wang Zhaojun was sent to a chieftain as a gift to keep the peace between his tribe and hers. Diaochan was chosen to mesmerize both a tyrant and his foster son and set them against each other. The Fourth Beauty, however, was blamed for bringing down the most glorious dynasty feudal China had ever known. Posterity remembers her as Yang Guifei. 楊 *Yang* is her family name, 貴 *gui* means "imperial" and 妃 *fei* means "consort". Yang Guifei's story has been repeatedly told in poems and novels, and reenacted in theaters as movies, television shows, and operas. The stories of Xishi and Wang Zhaojun will be told in some of the poems to follow. For now, let us get to know Yang Guifei a little better.

Yang Guifei 楊貴妃

She was born Yang Yuhuan in 719 to a minor official and was the youngest of four daughters. Her name, 玉環 Yuhuan, means "Jade Bracelet". Her parents both died when she was just a baby, and she and her sisters were raised by their uncle. She must have been extraordinarily beautiful even as a child, because the emperor's scouts spotted her and chose her to be wife to the Crown Prince Li Mao, one of the sons of Lady Wu. The emperor at the time was Tang Xuanzong, and Lady Wu was his Imperial Consort. In 733, Yang Yuhuan was brought to court and soon married to Li Mao. She was fourteen and he was thirteen. In 737, Lady Wu died. Emperor Xuanzong was despondent until, a year later, he noticed his son's wife and wanted her for himself.

It was not unusual for emperors to have many concubines, nor was it particularly remarkable for him to randomly pick a beauty out of a crowd and install her in his harem. Yang Yuhuan was, however, the Crown Prince's wife. To avoid gossip in court and to spare everyone's feelings, Xuanzong ordered Yang Yuhuan to the nunnery, and bestowed on her the Daoist name of *Taizhen* 太真 which means "Most True". By this time, Yuhuan was nineteen and Xuanzong fifty-one. For the next seven years, she was secretly ferried between temple and palace for rendezvous with the emperor. In 745, Li Mao finally took a new wife. Xuanzong now openly welcomed the Daoist nun to the palace. Before long, Yuhuan displaced the existing Imperial Consort. From then on, she was known as Yang Guifei, Imperial Consort Yang.

MY CHINA IN TANG POETRY

For the next eleven years, until her death at thirty-seven, the Yang family held sway. The Emperor's fondness for her extended to embrace the entire clan. Not only were her parents posthumously honored, but her three elder sisters were given titles as well. Nepotism, bribery, corruption and intrigue ran rampant. One cousin in particular, a drunk and a gambler, was able to worm his way into the emperor's good graces by becoming his gaming partner. Soon, he was made chancellor. His name was Yang Guozhong, an older cousin of the Yang sisters and paramour of Lady Guo, Yang Guifei's eldest sister.

As the Emperor's favorite, Yang Guifei enjoyed immeasurable luxury and countless indulgences. For example: the lychee was one of her favorite fruits, but it was grown only in the south and in season for a short time. To please her, Xuanzong ordered his fastest horsemen to ride down to the region every year to bring back this precious fruit as soon as news of its ripening arrived. Today, there is a species of lychees called "The Imperial Consort's Smile". Another example of his munificence towards her had to do with clothes. We are told that she had an assemblage of seven hundred silk weavers and skilled embroiderers who attended to refreshing her wardrobe.

We left Li Bai in the last chapter on his way to Chang'an. He was thirty-one. He made friends with a fellow Daoist and the older poet He Zhizhang 賀知章 on his way and traveled with him to the capital. He Zhizhang was the one who dubbed him "the poet the gods sent away" or "the banished immortal". He Zhizhang was not the only one who recognized Li Bai's enormous talent. Everything about Li Bai was big and dramatic. Others have conferred upon him such titles as "the drunk immortal" or "the god of poetry". On the negative side, he had offended many and was even said to have killed several people when, in his knight-errant persona, he fought to right the wrongs suffered by those who could not defend themselves. It was because of his colorful reputation that Emperor Xuanzong wanted to meet him, and on meeting was so impressed that he granted him a post in the Hanlin Academy, a kind of Imperial institute, which provided literary and scholarly expertise to the court. As the story goes, Emperor Xuanzong had allowed the poet to approach his royal person on their first meeting, and even served him soup from his own table! Entirely unheard of. The poet, for his part, was his usual arrogant self and did not submit to the conventions of palace life. Thus, despite this emperor's fondness and therefore lenience towards him, his good fortune did not last. Li Bai managed to insult quite a number of higher-ups, including the most powerful eunuch and general at the time, Gao Lishi 高力士. He was soon given the boot.

His downfall came after a feast that Xuanzong had prepared for Yang Guifei to celebrate the peony's blooming in one of the Imperial gardens. As usual, Li was dead drunk when the palace guards found him in town. He had to be rudely awakened, and in a foul mood, transported to the palace. When he arrived, the eunuch general, Gao Lishi, was one of the first to greet him. The poet stuck his muddy boot in the important man's face and asked him to take it off for him. The general was not amused, and soon after that night, persuaded Lady Yang to whisper in Emperor Xuanzong's ear and dismiss the poet from the Academy. From then on, Li Bai's unconventional behavior went from bad to worse and a couple of decades later, he was rumored to have accidentally killed himself in a drunken stupor by trying to scoop the moon out of a river.

Going back to the celebration that fateful evening, Li Bai was instructed to write a poem that simultaneously praised the flower in bloom, the peony, and the lady, Yang Guifei. Some readers have conjectured that this was the occasion of her birthday. First, some pre-reading information: 1) These are three *ci*-lyrics, a newly fashionable genre (see Endnote), so its Chinese title is that of the tune. I have given it my own title and called all three poems a suite. 2) Spring Wind comes from the East to China and is often personified as male, because it brings life. Here, this masculine wind can also imply the emperor himself. 3) Hills of Jade and Moon Jade Terrace are both heavenly residences of beautiful and immortal women. 4) The Tang Dynasty is often compared to the Han Dynasty (202 BCE – 220 CE), usually as a compliment. Here, Flying Swallow is also actually from the Han Dynasty. 5) The peony is often associated with wealth and celebrated by the Chinese. Kingdom's Fall 傾城 is idiom for a beautiful woman. It is the Chinese equivalent of "the face that launched a thousand ships". Its backstory will be told on the next few pages. King and emperor are not differentiated in the Chinese. I am therefore using the two words, king and emperor, interchangeably throughout this volume. And, finally, we are at Aloeswood Terrace on the Imperial Palace grounds, which he explicitly names in the last line.

A SUITE FOR MY LADY
To the Tune of 清平調, "A Clear and Level Tune"

> Clouds envy the clothes she wears; flowers want her face.
> Spring wind, laden with dew scent, rises to embrace her.
> Should you miss her among the stars on the Hills of Jade,
> come to Moon Jade Terrace where, for you, she is waiting.

SUPERSTARS

A luscious crimson branch: frozen scent mixed in dew.
Cloud and rain at Witch Mountain where hearts break.
Tell me who can compare to her in all of Han's palaces?
Perhaps only Flying Swallow, freshly made up at dawn.

Fêted flower, Kingdom's Fall, delighting each to each,
may he smile on you forever, you who can decipher
the spring wind's endless longing and infinite desire,
leaning on Aloeswood Terrace, late into the scented night.

清平調

雲想衣裳花想容，
春風拂檻露華濃。
若非羣玉山頭見，
會向瑤台月下逢。

一枝穠豔露凝香，
雲雨巫山枉斷腸。
借問漢宮誰得似，
可憐飛燕倚新妝。

名花傾國兩相歡，
長得君王帶笑看。
解釋春風無限恨，
沉香亭北倚闌干。

When he first recited the poem that evening, everyone applauded. In the light of day, Gao Lishi alerted Yang Guifei to the affront he found in the second stanza, in the comparison of her to Flying Swallow, the Han Emperor's famous consort, who was the fairest of them all in her own day. Portraits of

MY CHINA IN TANG POETRY

Yang Guifei show her to be voluptuously endowed, usually in low-cut, high-waisted flowing dresses fashionable at the time, whereas Flying Swallow was slim and a dancer. Now, in the Tang dynasty, lovely women with a bit of flesh were preferred over slender beauties, so there was no reason for Yang Guifei to feel diminished in the comparison, but that the poet dared even to mention another famous mortal beauty in the same breath was enough of an affront to warrant dismissal. Whether this story of aroused jealousy over a five-hundred-year-old rival was the cause of Li Bai's removal from the Hanlin Academy or not, is anyone's guess. At a time when people's heads were chopped off for minor offenses, though, he had gotten off easy for what were *really* hidden in these rich and sensual images.

The following are some of the barbs Gao Lishi missed. The opening line, "Clouds envy the clothes she wears," which at first glance was an extravagant compliment, can be read as criticism of her and her family's extravagance while their countrymen were starving. (Du Fu will have much to say about this in his poems). In Li Bai's poem, the mention of her clothes was most likely a reminder of her seven hundred weavers and embroiderers. Then there are the "Hills of Jade" and "Moon Jade Terrace". These are fairytale places where beautiful women are gathered, so one would think the poet was calling the Consort an immortal whose beauty was beyond comparison to mere earthlings. The allusion to Moon Jade Terrace, however, brings *Li Sao* to mind. The poet of that great work was Qu Yuan, often called the first poet-patriot of China, and *Li Sao* was his lament, bemoaning his emperor's wanton behavior and admonishing him to change his ways before it was too late. Also, Li Bai often identified himself with Qu Yuan. In any case, just by bringing the ancient poet to mind is enough for us to read it as a warning to the Tang emperor.

Witch Mountain is my translation of Wushan in the second

stanza, (*wu* 巫 is witch, , and *shan* 山 is mountain.) Geographically, this is a scenic area in the middle of China, but this is also a mountain in a fairytale where two different kings (respectively of the third and the fourth centuries BCE during the Chu period) dreamed that they made love to a beautiful lady who came in the form of cloud and rain and disappeared afterwards, never to return. Thereafter, the coupling of the two words, "cloud and rain" 雲雨, became a euphemism for intercourse. The juxtaposition of the Tang lovers to the ones on Wushan might be romantic, but surely not very auspicious for the present love affair, as the Wushan affairs alluded to were both illusory and short-lived.

Flying Swallow as mentioned earlier was another famous consort. She belonged to Emperor Cheng of the Han Dynasty. Her name, "Flying Swallow", came from the way she danced. She was as lovely as those flying acrobats, the swallows. In that story, Emperor Cheng fell in love with the dancer when he saw her perform, and soon, she and her sister were both brought into his harem. He became so enamored of Flying Swallow that he deposed his existing empress and installed the dancer in her place. Flying Swallow, however, was barren. For fear of losing the emperor's favor, she found ways to kill off all the other concubines' sons. In the end, Emperor Cheng was left with no heir and was succeeded by a nephew. When the nephew also died, the Wang Mang Rebellion erupted, and Flying Swallow was arrested. As an insult, she was made caretaker of Emperor Cheng's tomb. She committed suicide. Gao Lishi may in fact have underread Li Bai's venomous juxtaposition of the two beauties. Moreover, in retrospect, the An Lushan rebellion that brought Emperor Tang Xuanzong to his knees and precipitated the Tang Dynasty's downfall, was eerily foreshadowed by the Wang Mang Rebellion here, even though Li Bai could not have known that at this time.

MY CHINA IN TANG POETRY

In the third and last stanza, Li Bai brings us back to Xuanzong's palace where Aloeswood Terrace was located. The expression "Kingdom's Fall," came from Li Yannian, another Han personage, a brilliant musician and perhaps one-time lover of Emperor Wu (141 BCE – 87 BCE). Now this musician had a sister, who was to become Lady Li to Emperor Wu. And, as the story goes, it was a song that this brother composed and sang to Majesty that brought her to his attention. It is this song that gave us the expression "Kingdom's Fall" to mean peerless beauty. Li Bai was one of many poets who have used it, which was probably why it slipped past his audience as flattery of the lady and not a warning to the king. Here is the Han musician's song:

> There is a beauty in the North
> unlike any man has ever seen.
> Her glance can topple a city,
> one more look, and the kingdom falls.
> A kingdom's fall is surely worth the price
> to have known such a beauty once in a life.

Returning to Li Bai's poem, we can now clearly see that our poet was admonishing his Emperor while pretending to praise his Consort. "Spring wind" in the third line, comes from the east to China, and this life-giving wind is conventionally personified as male. Here, spring wind and emperor are one and the same. To be able to decipher the king's springtime longings was indeed the Imperial Consort's forte. This ability, however, was not only magical but somewhat menacing given the context of the entire poem.

The word for "longing" or "wanting" 恨, *hen*, (pronounced like *hun*,) found in the third line of the last stanza, is a shapeshifter, and therefore, slippery to translate. It means different things in different contexts, especially when it comes to love. As in our current usage of the word "bad", it can mean the opposite of itself. For example, (*wo hen ni*), "I hate you," can also mean "I love you so much that I hate you because you leave me forever wanting." The famous "Song of Everlasting Sorrow" (長恨歌 *Chang Hen Ge*), written more than half a century after Yang Gueifei's death, is about this Tang Emperor and his Imperial Consort. It is written by another Tang dynasty poet, Bai Juyi, and the word-for-word translation of the title is (*chang*) "long for forever," (*hen*) "longing/wanting" (*ge*) "song." This long poem has become the source of many Yang Guifei stories. Outside of China, this poem became especially popular among the aristocracy of mid-Heian period in Japan, which accounts for the numerous references to Bai Juyi and his poems in *The Tale of Genji* and other works of classical Japanese literature and paintings. In Japan, Bai Juyi is known by his courtesy name of Bai Letian, 白楽天, pronounced Hakurakuten in Japanese.

In Bai Juyi's narrative, we find the tragic conclusion to Yang Guifei who was blamed, rightly or wrongly, for the fall of the dynasty, or at least the beginnings of this kingdom's fall (see "The Big Picture", Chapter Six, for more historical background). Bai Juyi's poem was written in 806 in response to a friend's request after a sight-seeing visit to Ma Wei 馬嵬 (Ghost Rock in my translation), the spot where she was forced to hang herself. Bai Juyi himself saw seven changes of monarchs in his lifetime, all descendants of the Li family; it was a long descent. In the poem, Bai Juyi refers to Tang Xuanzong as the "King of Han". It seems, from the opening lines, that the poet had meant to condemn Xuanzong for his wanton pursuit of beauty. As he became caught up in the love story, however, his moral scruples were overtaken, and condemnation turned into admiration. His poem, which I am calling "Curse of Passion", is remembered by posterity more as a love story than a historical lesson. The reason for my play on the title will become clear as the poem progresses. In addition, in Volume III, we shall see the beginnings of this historical tale in Bai's own love story.

CURSE OF PASSION

The King of Han was a sensual man, bent on possessing
his Kingdom's Fall. For years he searched in vain
until one day he found her in the Yang family's care.
Raised in seclusion, the world had yet to set eyes on her.
Such beauty is born of heaven and would not be denied,
soon, she was chosen, and by the King, she took her place.
At the turn of her head, a smile, and none escaped her charm.
Ladies of all Six Palaces grew pale by her side.
Early in spring he had the Pool of Blossoms prepared:
hot spring water rolled off her creamy flesh like pearls
till half-leaning on palace maids she emerged,
sultry and beguiling, she won the king's heart.
Her hair like clouds, her face like a flower,
her golden steps held sway. Behind lotus bed-curtains
warm nights of spring were spent. Spring nights are short
and mornings hard to catch: the king no longer attended
early audience, his nights were used up in play. Not a day
passed without a celebration as spring followed spring
    laughter
and night turned to night. Three thousand beauties awaited
their lover, his favors for three thousand lavished on one.[2]
For her he fashioned a golden palace, for him she banished
    night,

---

2   That is, the number of beauties he collected in his harem.

when feasts at jade pavilions were over, feasts of passion
 began.
Her sisters and brothers filled all the high places,
splendid gifts light up their once humble doors.
Throughout the kingdom parents were saying,
not sons, but daughters, were worth much more.
Above Black Horse Ridges, tall spires pierced purple clouds.
Immortal music drifting through the air reached mortal ears
 everywhere.
Flow of songs, threads of dance, spun a web of silk and
 bamboo trance.
All for the king's pleasure, the days were never long enough.
Without warning, war drums of Yu Yang shook the earth,
scattering the dance of "Feather Smocks and Rainbow Skirts."[3]
Outside Ninefold City Gates, smoke and dust rose high,
thousands of carts and horses cluttered the southwest sky.
Imperial banners trembled in the wind, faltering onward,
leaving the capital behind. Only thirty miles out of the city,
all six regiments refused to move on. What could the King do
but grant their wish, the wish of soldiers immune to her allure.
She yielded to their call, and reeling before their horses, died.
Her golden headdress fell to the ground for no one to claim.
The king covered his face, knowing he could not save her,
and when he turned to look, blood and tears intermingled.
Yellow sand would not settle in the biting, soughing wind.
They crossed Twin Blades' hanging bridges and climbed over
 clouds.
Below the cliffs of Moth Brow Ranges there were few
 passersby.
His royal banners lost their color, the sky grew dim.

---

[3] Xuanzong was supposed to have composed the music and Yang Guifei choreographed the dance. This piece of music is lost to us.

MY CHINA IN TANG POETRY

The waters of Shu are green,[4] the mountains of Shu are blue,
the chill of dawn and dusk suffused the monarch's longing.
A cold moon shone on his imperial camp, breaking his heart,
through the night rain a distant bell reminded him of her voice.
And the sky rolled round, and the earth came full circle,
and the imperial train returned to the place where his love was lost
on the muddy slopes of Ghost Rock.[5] He hesitated, unable to move on.
She lay under this indifferent mud, with nothing to mark the spot.
The king and his ministers looked at each other as tears silently fell.
Turning east to the city gates, they let their horses take them home.
Returning to the familiar, to the Pond of Lotus Dripping Dew,
to the Evergreen Hall in the Willow's Shade, he saw her face
in the lotus flower, her brows in the willow's yielding branches.
Everywhere he looked she was there. How could his tears not fall?
On nights when spring blossoms were teased open by the wind,
or when, in autumn, the rain fell furiously on wutong trees,[6]
the king laid awake. In his royal residence grass grew wild.
Fallen leaves remained upswept, red petals covered the steps.
Apprentice actors in Pear Garden counted new white hairs,

---

4   Twin Blades, Moth Brow Ranges trace the route they took. Xuanzong had fled to Shu in the south.
5   Ghost Rock is Mawei 馬嵬 where the character for *wei* is written as a mountain radical on top of the word for ghost 鬼.
6   Wutong 梧桐 is a tree with green trunks and large parasol-like leaves.

and ladies-in-waiting in Pepper Rooms watched their brows fade.
At nightfall, fireflies and memories stole into the silent corridors,
and in his room, he sat alone, trimming the wick of a dying lamp.
The hour-drum struck early; the long nights persisted.
Stubborn stars struggled to keep the sky from dawning.
Mandarin ducks huddled together in the heavy morning frost.
Who was there to hold the king, to keep his kingfisher quilt warm?
So great the distance that separates the dead from the living,
another year had passed and still her ghost was denied his dreams.
A Taoist priest from Lingqiong, a medium who could reach spirits
by his sincerity, was summoned to the capital.
Moved by the king's longing, he agreed to help him find her.
Fast as lightning he rode the air, parting clouds,
combing the heavens above and the earth below,
but neither in the rarified heights of Green Heaven
nor in the nether world of Yellow Spring was there
any trace of her, until a voice from nowhere revealed
that there was a magic mountain far out in the sea,
where pavilions rose like crystals on rainbow clouds,
and among the radiant faces of the immortal beauties,
there was one whose skin was softer than snow and whose face
was like a flower, and she was the one they called Most True.
He arrived then before a golden gate and knocked on the palace door.

MY CHINA IN TANG POETRY

Soon, fairy maids appeared one after another to announce his arrival.
Behind Nine Flower bed-curtains she had dreamed the news:
from the House of Han, his messenger had at last come to call.
Startled from her dreams, not fully awake,
she pushed her pillows aside and straightened her robe.
Pearl curtains and silver veils opened one by one:
headdress rumpled, chignon undone, fresh from sleep she came.
The wind played on her sleeves, lifting them, as if
still to the dance of "Feather Smocks and Rainbow Skirts."
Her face like a lone white flower, tears about to fall,
she was like a branch of pear blossoms dressed in spring and rain.
Holding back her tears, she thanked her king for not forgetting her:
"Once parted, the living from the dead, faces, voices, are hard to recall.
Those days at the Morning Sun, when our love seemed eternal,
are not as long as the endless days here in eternal heaven.
Each time I turn to look on the circle-of-dust below,
I see only a veil of mist covering the capital, Chang'an.
All I have are these objects now to convey my feelings.
Here is a gold casket and a golden hairpin too, take one side
of each of these treasures and let them speak of our love.
If our hearts can learn their lessons, like gold we will endure,
and the day will come when the sky above meets the earth below."
As the priest took his leave, she repeated her words more urgently,

and in her words, she hid a promise that only their two hearts knew.
On the Seventh Day of the Seventh Month, at the Palace of Eternity,
in the middle of the night, they whispered to each other this private vow:
we'll fly in the air like those fabulous birds who share one pair of wings,
we'll grow from the earth like twin branches out of the self-same tree.
The sky is long, the earth is old, but in time they too will end.
This unfinished web of passion will spin till time is spent.

The Seventh Day of the Seventh Month when they made their vow, is the festival day celebrating the unending but forbidden love between the immortal Weaver and the mortal Cowherd which we shall come across often in other Chinese poems. In the end, they were metamorphosed into two stars, known in the West as Venus and Altair, but allowed to come together once a year.

長恨歌

漢皇重色思傾國，御宇多年求不得。
楊家有女初長成，養在深閨人未識。
天生麗質難自棄，一朝選在君王側。
回眸一笑百媚生，六宮粉黛無顏色。
春寒賜浴華清池，溫泉水滑洗凝脂。
侍兒扶起嬌無力，始是新承恩澤時。
雲鬢花顏金步搖，芙蓉帳暖度春宵。
春宵苦短日高起，從此君王不早朝。
承歡侍宴無閒暇，春從春遊夜專夜。

MY CHINA IN TANG POETRY

後宮佳麗三千人，三千寵愛在一身。
金屋妝成嬌侍夜，玉樓宴罷醉和春。
姊妹弟兄皆列土，可憐光彩生門戶。
遂令天下父母心，不重生男重生女。
驪宮高處入青雲，仙樂風飄處處聞。
緩歌慢舞凝絲竹，盡日君王看不足。
漁陽鼙鼓動地來，驚破霓裳羽衣曲。
九重城闕煙塵生，千乘萬騎西南行。
翠華搖搖行復止，西出都門百餘里。
六軍不發無奈何，宛轉蛾眉馬前死。
花鈿委地無人收，翠翹金雀玉搔頭。
君王掩面救不得，回看血淚相和流。
黃埃散漫風蕭索，雲棧縈紆登劍閣。
峨嵋山下少人行，旌旗無光日色薄。
蜀江水碧蜀山青，聖主朝朝暮暮情。
行宮見月傷心色，夜雨聞鈴腸斷聲。
天旋地轉回龍馭，到此躊躇不能去。
馬嵬坡下泥土中，不見玉顏空死處。
君臣相顧盡沾衣，東望都門信馬歸。
歸來池苑皆依舊，太液芙蓉未央柳。
芙蓉如面柳如眉，對此如何不淚垂？
春風桃李花開日，秋雨梧桐葉落時。
西宮南內多秋草，落葉滿階紅不掃。
梨園弟子白髮新，椒房阿監青娥老。
夕殿螢飛思悄然，孤燈挑盡未成眠。
遲遲鐘鼓初長夜，耿耿星河欲曙天。
鴛鴦瓦冷霜華重，翡翠衾寒誰與共？
悠悠生死別經年，魂魄不曾來入夢。
臨邛道士鴻都客，能以精誠致魂魄。
為感君王輾轉思，遂教方士殷勤覓。
排空馭氣奔如電，昇天入地求之遍。
上窮碧落下黃泉，兩處茫茫皆不見。

忽聞海上有仙山，山在虛無縹緲間。
樓閣玲瓏五雲起，其中綽約多仙子。
中有一人字太真，雪膚花貌參差是。
金闕西廂叩玉扃，轉教小玉報雙成。
聞道漢家天子使，九華帳裏夢魂驚。
攬衣推枕起徘徊，珠箔銀屏迤邐開。
雲鬢半偏新睡覺，花冠不整下堂來。
風吹仙袂飄飄舉，猶似霓裳羽衣舞。
玉容寂寞淚闌干，梨花一枝春帶雨。
含情凝睇謝君王，一別音容兩渺茫。
昭陽殿裏恩愛絕，蓬萊宮中日月長。
回頭下望人寰處，不見長安見塵霧。
惟將舊物表深情，鈿合金釵寄將去。
釵留一股合一扇，釵擘黃金合分鈿。
但教心似金鈿堅，天上人間會相見。
臨別殷勤重寄詞，詞中有誓兩心知。
七月七日長生殿，夜半無人私語時。
在天願作比翼鳥，在地願為連理枝。
天長地久有時盡，此恨綿綿無絕期。

The word *chang* 長 in *Chang Hen Ge*, 長恨歌, "Song of *Everlasting* Sorrow," is also the word in *Chang*'an, 長安, the capital, or Chang Jiang, 長江, the Yangtze, and the many *Chang Xiang Si*, 長相思 "Thinking of You" poems we find in Chinese poetry. The word *chang* is tremendously resonant in Chinese, where it almost sounds like a sigh. Used with life, for example, as in 長命, long life, it is a happy sigh; used with sadness or regret, as in 長恨, everlasting sorrow, it is a sad sigh.

3

From Palace to Wilderness (Part I)

In his chapter, "Political Involvement," Ha Jin described the incident that finally gave Li Bai the title of "Royal Secretary of the Fifth Rank", and a good salary as a translator to the court, because, on a chance occasion, he happened to recognize a foreign script from the western frontier. Before long though, his brilliance, which invited envy, and his arrogance and drunkenness had made him enough powerful enemies that he feared for his life. In 744, he petitioned to leave the capital, probably soon after the peony celebration. History is a little vague on the exact reason, although the Gao Lishi rumor is a plausible explanation. Xuanzong, knowing how his top ministers disliked the poet, accepted Li Bai's petition, gave him some gold bars, and sent him off. With great dramatic flourish, Li Bai made a display of leaving worldly cares for the spiritual life of a Daoist and even went as far as to don the Daoist black hat and cloak as he rode out of the capitol gate, accompanied by his many friends.

Predictably, he did not head straight home to his children, instead he headed for the legend-laden, beautiful coast where the story of Xishi took place. This, you might remember, was his first destination when he left home as a young man of twenty-three. I am speaking of Shanzhong, where the ancient story of Wu 吳 and Yue 越 took place.

SUPERSTARS

Xishi 西施

Xishi enters this ancient tale of rivalry, revenge, obsession, and determination late. To start at the beginning of it all, we have to return to a runaway princess. Who knows why she ran away, maybe she was homesick. She was from the neighboring state of Yue and given in marriage to the Prince of Wu. The incident did not help matters between the two states and fanned the flames between them that the marriage was supposed to calm. The initial confrontation took place during the period of turmoil recorded in the *Spring and Autumn Annals* (c.771 - c.476 BCE). And eventually concluded with the Battle of Zuli. Yue won this first battle in defense of the princess, and mortally wounded the king of Wu who, with his dying breath, said to his son, Fuchai, 夫差 "NEVER FORGET YUE." This was the Battle of Zuli. Meanwhile, the King of Yue also died, and his son, Goujian 勾践 ascended the throne. We are now into the second generation of warring kings.

A few years later, Fuchai indeed came back to avenge his father and soundly defeated Goujian. In the end, only 5,000 Yue men survived. Goujian, facing defeat, bribed Fuchai's chancellor to help him negotiate the terms for his surrender, and because Fuchai was more interested in the states further north to Yue, agreed to not annex Yue but simply take Goujian captive. When Fuchai withdrew from Yue, Goujian brought his wife and right-hand man, Fan Li, to the Wu court to be servants to Fuchai as promised. He himself volunteered to work in the stables. They were at Wu for three years. During that time, Fuchai fell very ill at one point, and Goujian was reputed to have gone to him, saying he had knowledge of medicine, and even went so far as to taste Fuchai's stool in order to diagnose his illness. That time, he came up with the prognosis that the King of Wu would live. When Fuchai recovered, he was grateful. Goujian's humility and diligence paid off, and Fuchai set him free to return to Yue.

MY CHINA IN TANG POETRY

For the next ten years (some say twenty), Goujian improved his government with the help of his chancellor, Wen Zhong, and built up his army with the help of his general, Fan Li, while working with the commoners to gain their loyalty, farming the fields himself while his wife worked with the weavers. To remind himself of the humiliation of defeat, he refused to sleep in his palace, but rather lay on a pile of spiny firewood in the stable and hung a piece of pig's gallbladder above his head, sleeping with a sword by his side. First thing each morning, he would sit up and taste the bitter gallbladder before he went about the day's task. In this way, he reminded himself of the bitterness of defeat, inspired his people, and readied them for war. Posterity will remember this practice with the proverb, 卧薪嚐胆, *wo xin chang dan,* "sleeping on firewood and tasting gall," to signify determination. After ten years of reform and hard work and generously rewarding his fighters for their allegiance, Goujian was ready for revenge. The Yue army was said to be so loyal that they would "charge in the face of arrows like thirsty men heading for water" (as recorded in the Sima Qian's *Shiji, Historical Records*).

Xishi enters the story as part of Goujian's preparation for war. He sent his top general, Fan Li, 范蠡, to look for the most alluring creature in his kingdom. Fan Li discovered her in her native Zhu Luo Hills while she was washing clothes by the river. The romantic among us said they fell in love. Xishi was described as so perfect that if she were half an inch taller, she would be too tall, half an inch shorter and she would be too short, and the same applied to everything about her person: she was perfect with or without makeup, dressed up or down. Later, when she became the King of Wu's concubine, she was reputed to be even more beautiful when she was drunk than sober, a hard thing to do. Plus, there was her inimitable frown that was supposed to make her even more beguiling. In any case, to continue with the lore, Fan Li brought her back to the palace and trained her to please in every imaginable way. At the same time, she was taught to be a spy. Goujian then sent her to Wu as a gift to Fuchai, whom he knew was fond of lovely women and would be easily distracted from statecraft by this heavenly addition to his harem. Goujian was not wrong. So, when Yue attacked, Wu toppled. Xishi, however, was never seen again in Yue, which added to her mystique. Some say she sailed off with Fan Li and lived quietly ever after. Some say she committed suicide.

In many poems of ancient China, young women's teeth are admired for the obvious reason that dentistry was, at best, a primitive art, and pretty teeth only belonged to the young and the fortunate few who were born with perfect pearly whites. In this case, Li Bai was also alluding to Xishi being quiet and decorous, i.e., she did not open her mouth wide to talk or laugh and show her teeth.

IN PRAISE OF XISHI OF THE ZHU LUO HILLS

Xishi was a washer maid of Yue,
sprung from the Zhu Luo Hills.
No one before or after her has equaled her in charm.
Waterlilies hide their faces for fear of being shamed.
Making ripples on the emerald water as she worked,
she was as supple as the gentle waves she aroused.
She was quiet and graceful as the floating clouds,
and her brilliant white teeth were hardly ever seen.
When her king needed the help of an extraordinary beauty,
she answered the call and departed for the Gates of Wu.
She became Fuchai's treasured captive, hidden away
in his Palace of Beauties, he kept her all to himself.
Once Fuchai was defeated, she was never seen again.

MY CHINA IN TANG POETRY

詠苧蘿山／西施

西施越溪女，出自苧蘿山。
秀色掩今古，荷花羞玉顏。
浣紗弄碧水，自與清波閒。
皓齒信難開，沉吟碧雲間。
勾踐徵絕艷，揚蛾入吳關。
提攜館娃宮，杳渺詎可攀。
一破夫差國，千秋竟不還。

This poem shows us what Li Bai admired about a person. It is interesting too that in one of his later poems, he called himself Xishi. In other words, for Li Bai, these desirable qualities were not confined to women. First, she was from the mountains, in the remote countryside. Secondly, she had no equal. These were obvious parallels to how Li Bai viewed himself. And not only was she pure and uncorrupted, but she was also brave and capable and completed her mission successfully. No doubt, her reputation as a drunken beauty also endeared her to him. Moreover, instead of returning to Yue for rewards and acclaim, she disappeared, like a Daoist immortal. Of all the admirable traits mentioned, this last might be what was most praiseworthy and perhaps enviable to Li Bai, as he, despite his many protestations, was yet to achieve that state of mind of not needing acclaim.

Goujian's story is made even more compelling to the modern Chinese by the discovery of his sword in 1965 in Hubei. It is now kept in a museum and considered a National Treasure. This is not the sword with which he fought Fuchai but the sword that, according to convention, was forged when he won. Apparently, after 2,400 years, the sword was discovered in perfect condition in a damp tomb and still razor sharp. It was lying by his bones, in a water-tight box. The next three poems were probably written either during Li Bai's first visit to the area when he was a young man in his twenties or after he left Chang'an in 744 as he wandered in the scenic spots visiting historical sites. Dating, as is often the case with Li Bai, is unreliable. And although the three poems below were not written as a suite, and they might not even have been written at the same time, they have the same setting and historical background. Thus, I have gathered them together.

The first two poems are seven-character *juejus*, also informed by the above story. The Kingdom of Yue and the Kingdom of Wu were situated in the delta region by the coast of China in today's Suzhou, famous for its canals, bridges, and gardens. This whole area is a bit like Venice where waterways surround buildings that almost look as if they are sitting on the water. The first poem is about Fuchai, the King of Wu, and the second is remembering the Kingdom of Yue, Goujian's palaces. The theme of both poems is much the same. In the first poem we find what are called bat nuts, so-called because they are black and take the shape of bats. Bat nuts are water caltrops that grow abundantly on the lake below the terrace and are edible. Water caltrop gatherers sing as they gather the seeds of these floating plants.

GUSU TERRACE REMEMBERED

> Long forsaken, this old park and terrace, only willows are fresh and new,
> bat nut gatherers sing a clear song as they row on the spring waters below.
> Is the West River moon the only one who can remember how it used to be,
> when it shone on the Wu King and his splendid palaces full of pretty maids?

MY CHINA IN TANG POETRY

蘇臺覽古

舊苑荒臺楊柳新，
菱歌清唱不勝春。
只今惟有西江月，
曾照吳王宮裏人。

REMEMBERING THE KINGDOM OF YUE

Home from thrashing Wu, the King of Yue granted generous gifts
to his soldiers, every man wore brocade back to his village. Then,
Goujian's palaces were filled with spring flowers and pretty maids.
Now, there are only a few quail here and there, trying to fly away.

越中覽古

越王勾踐破吳歸，
義士還家盡錦衣。
宮女如花滿春殿，
只今惟有鷓鴣飛。

The next poem is "The Crow Roosting Song". It takes its title from an original Six Dynasties (220–589 ACE) *yuefu* that Li Bai was "imitating," that is, taking the verse form without copying its content. Moreover, it is a so-called "western tune" and usually used to celebrate passion and romance. Here, Li Bai is doing the opposite with it and using the tune to underline the stark difference between the glory days of Wu and Yue and the desolation of the present. The original tune also had eight lines of seven-characters each, so, at first glance, it looks like a *lushi*. To a Chinese reader or listener who is expecting eight lines for a *lushi*, the poem ends abruptly with seven lines. The effect is that of something curtailed. It is as if one is cut off mid-sentence. It has the effect of an utterance which reenacts the abrupt ending of Fuchai's parties, like a song coming to a sudden break by the unstoppable movement of time and events, specifically for this King of Wu, by being brought to his knees by his enemy. Since we do not have that built-in expectation of eight-line verses in English, to produce the effect of Li Bai's unexpectedly abrupt ending, I have allowed my lines to get longer and longer to produce the illusion of time being lengthened by the King of Wu's endless parties, until it is cut short in the truncated last line. He Zhizhang, the older poet who dubbed Li Bai "the banished immortal", was apparently so moved by this poem when he heard it that he copied it out by hand and passed it on to everyone he met, saying that it was so touching that it can make ghosts weep. Notice that the poem starts in early evening, when crows roost, and ends at sunrise, instead of the other way around as might be expected of a poem about the ending of days.

MY CHINA IN TANG POETRY

A CROW ROOSTING SONG

When crows roost at Gusu Terrace
in King Wu's Palace, Xishi is already drunk.
Songs of Wu and dances from Chu are still twirling on
even as the green mountain has already devoured half the sun,
and the silver arrow on the gold water-clock is about to point straight down.
If the King would open his eyes, he'd see that the autumn moon is sinking fast into the ocean,
but what can be done about the rising sun?

烏棲曲

姑蘇臺上烏棲時，吳王宮裡醉西施。
吳歌楚舞歡未畢，青山欲銜半邊日。
銀箭金壺漏水多，起看秋月墜江波。
東方漸高奈樂何！

    I imagine the silver arrow to be like the hand of our clocks; when it points downward it is ready to move back up as the sun rises? In the poem, however, this downward pointing is ominous. Also, the penultimate line in the Chinese reads: "If the King would get up and look." I left him lounging as it would make my line too long if he got up. Either way, the result is the same: he'd see the error of his ways.
    The next poem is called "The Road to Shu is Hard". Its date of composition is unclear, except that it had to have been written before 753 as it was included in one of the collections that came out at that time. Most commentators agree that it was written sometime between 742 and 744. In other words, just before, during, or right after his trip to Chang'an to report to duty at the Palace.

SUPERSTARS

A small portion of this poem has been imbedded into a Chinese rap as performed by the singer Jason Zhang Jie in his rock concert of 2018. As with quite a number of popular songs, not necessarily rap, lines from Tang poems are written into modern lyrics, and some poems are simply set to music. This poem is emblematic and is often read simply as a landscape or mountain poem, but the more I read it, the more I find it to be far more than scenic, and as Jason Zhang Jieh would surely agree, it is definitely a boast!

Some ideas for the reading of "The Road to Shu is Hard":

Shu 蜀 is ancient tribal territory in today's Sichuan. In 1987, an important archeological discovery at Sanxingdui 三星堆, forty kilometers north of Chengdu, the capital of Sichuan, dates it as existing from c. 2050-1250 BCE. In Tang times, that is, almost two thousand years later, the territory had become part of China. At that time, Sichuan was still generally referred to as Shu. Today, there are still fifty-five ethnic minorities in Sichuan.[7] Li Bai knew nothing of Sanxingdue, of course, but he knew the old classics and records of Han very well, which means he knew the mythology and history of the area.

As we know, Li Bai was born in Central Asia (today's Kyrgyzstan) in Suyab and his mother was not Chinese, but Turkic. His father, Li Ke had secretly moved the family south from Suyab to Jiangyou, which was near Chengdu, in Sichuan. China, at the time, was the dominant country in Asia. Who wouldn't want to be Chinese or Han? And if one were Chinese in the Tang dynasty, short of being in the Imperial family, the next best thing would be to become a scholar-official in the Imperial Court.

We also know that Li Bai was a gifted child and knew all

---

7   This Shu state is not the same as the one referred to also as Shu in the Three Kingdoms Period (220-280). To differentiate between the two, we call the latter, Shu Han, because its founder, Liu Bei, lays claim to being the legitimate heir of the Han Dynasty, which fell apart before the Three Kingdoms rose. Shu Han existed from 221-263 and was based in Sichuan as well. Thus, the confusion. This is also the area where Xuanzong, the Tang emperor, escaped to when An Lushan took over his capital.

the classics by age ten. Apparently, he was also strikingly good-looking. It was said that he looked "foreign", but in an attractive kind of way, not like the hairy and rotund An Lushan, for example. Remember the story about Venus falling to earth at his birth? From the beginning, there was a certain mystique about him, even in his own family. He was the twelfth child among his brothers, and because of his extraordinary intelligence, the obvious choice for his father's own aspirations to elevate the family in Chinese society. Thus, this twelfth son was groomed to be a scholar-official even though his other brothers had to follow in the father's footsteps to become merchant-traders and make money for the family. In other words, Li Bai was aware of three things from a very young age: 1) he was chosen for great deeds, by his father, if not by heaven itself, and the reminder was written right there in his name, 2) though his father claimed to be descended from the great general Li Guang (184-119 BCE), and therefore distantly related to Tang's royal family, he and his siblings were, nevertheless "foreigners", or at least half-foreigners, and may even be "illegals", and 3) the family's aspiration for glory was squarely laid on his shoulders.

Imagine the conflict of being a half-caste son of a merchant and yet more learned than the average Han Chinese scholar. Imagine being looked down on by those who wished for his failure, either due to snobbery or envy. Imagine, not only was he educated in more ways than one and a superb poet, but he was also a swordsman and Daoist, and wandered through so much of the country that he knew it better than most Han Chinese generals. Imagine then, being vilified and rejected by in-laws and people in power and people who were so much inferior to himself. Is it any wonder he was so frustrated and half-crazed? Any wonder that his boastfulness and self-invention went through the roof? Any wonder he chose to escape to the nether sphere of alcohol as often as he seemed to have done? Given this background, it seems to me that Li Bai's identity with the mountains, or Shu in this poem, is obvious. Like the mountains of Shu, he, too was awe-inspiring and difficult to fathom, and even though he claimed to be an honest-to-goodness Han Chinese poet, nevertheless, Shu blood coursed in his veins, or, more accurately, his mother's foreign blood coursed in his veins.

"The Road to Shu" is hard, and if you can make it out of here, you can make it anywhere, the poem seems to say, and he had made it out. "*Yi xu xi*" is a Shu expression meaning *OMG* as young people these days might say. It is an expression of awe, of disbelief, of surprise, of defiance even. The poem opens with "Silkworm" or "Silkworm Bushes" and "Cormorant," two mythic kings at the founding of Shu, *not quite* "forty-eight thousand years [ago]". At the end of this movement, where he repeats "the road to Shu is hard," we find Duyu, another Shu king, who was turned into a cuckoo. Duyu, however, had by this time, appeared in many poems and seemed to have been incorporated into Han mythology. In any case, in the days of these mythological kings, Shu was at the edge of China, looking in on that "superior" Han culture.

The Han culture originated from the Yellow River Basin in the northeast, when the State of Chu expanded westward in the fifth and fourth century BCE. At the same time, the Ba people were pushed into the Shu area. Ba was on the east of Shu; Chu (i.e. Han) is on the east of Ba. Archeologists speak of a Ba-Shu culture at this time where some Chu influence could also be found. Surrounded by mountains, this area, now called the Sichuan Basin, was isolated from what was then China. Eventually, the Qin Dynasty (221-206 BCE) swallowed everyone up and united it all into one country. All this to say, for the purpose of my thesis, when we come across Ba, Shu, and Chu in Li Bai's poetry, we should not forget that he spent his childhood years in the Ba-Shu region.

> To continue, lines 6 and 7 read:
> Sheltered by these mountains, unknown to Qin [meaning China].
> On their west, lies Taibai, bird's path through the mountains,

A word-for-word reading of line 6 produces: "Does not communicate/cross over the borders of Qin." "Unknown to Qin," therefore, is a good thing because that was why it did not, at first, tempt Qin (the Han people) to absorb it into their territory. "Taibai," in the next line, happens to be a real place, Mount Taibai, named after the star. "Bird's path" is what the Chinese call the dip between two crests, as if the mountains were making way for the birds to fly through. Here, Taibai was providing such an outlet. Whether the use of Taibai here is simply incidental, we cannot ignore the fact that it is the poet's courtesy name, and he must have meant something by using it, or at least it must have meant something to him.

"The strong men of Shu," were from a story found in the third century's *Book of Shu*: Wei, King of Qin, wanted to find a way to take Shu and offered to send five beautiful women to the Shu king to distract him, having heard that that was his weakness (seems like a common strategy and common weakness). The King of Shu then offered to send five of his strong young men to go and escort the beauties home. On their way, as they were just south of Double Blade Pass, one of the men saw a great snake and ran into a cave after it, grabbed its tail, and called to the other four men to help him pull it out. Before long, the mountain caved in and the ground split apart, and braves and ladies were all buried alive. From then on, the road into Shu was opened. A variant of the story is that the five men dug canals and regulated the floods coming from the mountains. All this information is from the *Shuwang Benji* or *Biographies of the Shu Kings* of the Former Han period (206 BCE-6 CE). From it is also found the story that Laozi, the original master of Daoism, had passed by these parts on his way to heaven. Apparently, he was about to ascend to heaven but was persuaded to first go to Chengdu, the capital of Shu. Li Bai was a keen follower of Daoism, and his fondness for mountains is found everywhere in his poetry. To him, it would seem, Heaven is just a step or climb away from the peaks, and if you have gone to China or seen Chinese mountain paintings, or photographs, you might agree. From here on, consult footnotes for more stories.

THE ROAD TO SHU IS HARD

Yi – xu – xi! Treacherous indeed, these rugged heights!
The road to Shu is hard, harder than climbing the clear blue
  sky!
Silkworm and Cormorant, founders of Shu, lost in time,
nestled in these mountains for forty-eight thousand years.
For all that time, Shu was hidden from Qin's hungry eyes.
On the west is Taibai, bird-path through the mountains,
lone crossing between the peaks of Moth Brow Ranges,
until Shu's strong men died, cracking the earth, molding the
  cliffs,
to join sheer steps and stone bridges, forming walkways in
  the sky.
The Six-Dragon Chariot[8] lands on its highest rock.
Whirlpools toss and tumble, pounding at its feet.

---

8   The Six-Dragon Chariot is the sun, driven by an emperor. The landing here means sunset.

White-haired snow-geese were stymied in their flight;[9]
yellow monkeys of Shu scratch their heads mid-climb.
Mudslides crash mightily into its cavernous platters,
nine coils wound tight, round its precipitous crown.
Hold your breath and touch the Stars of Shu and Qin,[10]
take a rest and reach out to pet the eagle by your side.
Ah-h, when will you be returning from your journey to the west?
Or are you trapped in these fearsome crags and cannot escape?
All you can hear are sorrowful birds, crying in ancient woods,
female following male as they circle round and round.
And from the darkness comes the cuckoo's call,[11]
sadder than the lonely moon.
The road to Shu is hard, harder than climbing the clear blue sky!
Rosy cheeks blanch at the mention of its name,
clouds twist and swirl round its mountain range.
Aged pines hang upside-down jutting from its sheer rock face,
waterfalls tearing off bluffs, clash and clang, one louder than the next,
rocks ground to crystals, splash and beat, like thunder on hollowed rocks.
Be warned, you adventurers,

---

9   These snow geese can fly at extreme heights; yellow monkeys of Shu are the best climbers. In other words, even they have trouble navigating these heights.
10 The map of the sky is supposed to correspond to that of the earth, which is why you can "read" the sky and predict what happens on earth. Thus, there is a Star of Shu and a Star of Qin representing them, respectively.
11 Another King of Shu, Wang Di is supposed to have been a god who transformed into a mortal to marry Lady Li. He appointed the wise Bie Ling as his counsellor but later had an affair with Bie's wife, which he regretted, thus turning himself into a cuckoo. The cuckoo's call sounded like *bu ru gui qu*, 不如歸去, "should've gone back," to the Chinese ear.

braving such distance for no good cause, think again before you set out!
Double Blades,[12] lofty and strategic, Nature's defense:
a single man standing guard
can keep a thousand at bay.
Not even family can be trusted here.
Who will not turn jackal or wolf?
Many before you have attempted to escape
fierce tigers at dawn and giant snakes at dusk:
they are sharpening their teeth,
waiting to drink your blood.
Even though people say Chengdu is a place for pleasure,
better think twice before you decide to stay another night.
The road to Shu is hard, harder than climbing the clear blue sky!
Turn around, take a deep breath, and say goodbye to the west![13]

蜀道難

噫籲嚱，危乎高哉！
蜀道之難，難於上青天！
蠶叢及魚鳧，開國何茫然！
爾來四萬八千歲，
不與秦塞通人煙。
西當太白有鳥道，
可以橫絕峨眉巔。
地崩山摧壯士死，

---

[12] Double Blade, (in Chinese, sword terrace, sometimes translated as double-edged sword) is a narrow pass that looks like the double sleeves of a door, which is why he says one man can fight a thousand, and therefore that one man can easily be tempted to take over the territory for himself, even if he is a member of the royal clan.

[13] The capital is to the East.

MY CHINA IN TANG POETRY

然後天梯石棧相鉤連。
上有六龍回日之高標,
下有衝波逆折之回川。
黃鶴之飛尚不得過,
猿猱欲度愁攀援。
青泥何盤盤,
百步九折縈巖巒。
捫參歷井仰脅息,
以手撫膺坐長嘆。
問君西遊何時還?
畏途巉巖不可攀。
但見悲鳥號古木,
雄飛雌從繞林間。
又聞子規啼夜月,
愁空山。
蜀道之難,難於上青天,
使人聽此凋朱顏!
連峯去天不盈尺,
枯松倒掛倚絕壁。
飛湍瀑流爭喧豗,
砯崖轉石萬壑雷。
其險也如此,
嗟爾遠道之人胡爲乎來哉!
劍閣崢嶸而崔嵬,
一夫當關,
萬夫莫開。
所守或匪親,
化爲狼與豺。
朝避猛虎,
夕避長蛇,
磨牙吮血,
殺人如麻。

SUPERSTARS

錦城雖雲樂,
不如早還家。
蜀道之難,難於上青天,
側身西望長咨嗟!

Li Bai is often described as a free spirit, a wanderer who preferred the company of mountains to that of men and even less so, family. His love for the moon and drinking, especially in the mountains, is legend. He was, however, not a loner. For as much time as he spent wandering the wilderness, his longing for company when he was alone can be seen everywhere in his poetry. The moon often brought on his thoughts of home, which meant both his family in Shu as well as his wife, especially the first one, and later, his children in the middle of China. He has written a few famous solitary drinking poems, but he seems to be most happy drinking with friends, and sometimes, lovers, and sometimes accompanied by sword dancing and poetry performances, either sung or dashed across a scroll with a calligraphy brush. Even his wandering in the wilderness, visits to the mountains, had a purpose, usually in search of immortals; immortals who were hermits or Daoist ecclesiastics. My reading then does not give me the feeling that he was as "aloof" or "pure" as some critics have presented him. Not to say that he did not have lofty thoughts and ambitious yearnings, but he was neither saint nor recluse. We love him so much precisely because he was all too human. As mentioned earlier, Li Bai was an intensely conflicted man, and the extremes of Daoist and Confucian philosophies are always present in his mind. We might call it the Yin and the Yang of him.

4

Drinking Songs

The following five drinking songs are some of the best known of Li Bai's poems and paints the picture of the clichéd drunken genius some like to imagine that he was.

At the end of the second of the two "By Moonlight" poems below, he brings up "Confucius' Way" and "Laozi's Nature", they are at the center of Confucian and Daoist teachings respectively.

BY MOONLIGHT, DRINKING ALONE (Two from a set of four)

> Among the flowers I feast alone
> on a jug of wine, myself my party.
> Here's to the moon, come out for me.
> Together with my shadow, we make three.
> But the moon has no mind for getting drunk,
> and my shadow is just slave to my body.
> Not much fun this, but it will have to do,
> spring's not waiting for better company.
> So long as the moon stays, I will sing
> and dance till my shadow grows tipsy.
> Awake, we'll entertain each other.
> Drunk, we'll go our separate ways.
> Fellow travelers, we make no demands,
> perhaps we'll meet beyond the Milky Way.

SUPERSTARS

If wine were not loved in Heaven,
there would be no Wine Star.
If wine were not loved by the Earth,
there would be no Wine Spring.
Since Heaven and Earth both love wine,
loving wine must not offend the gods.
Light wines are called "saintly", I have heard,
and a heavy wine is often called "sage".
Since saints and sages are among us drinkers,
what need do we have for immortals?
Three cups and I can understand Confucius' Way,
a whole jug will take me back to Laozi's Nature.
All it takes is to have tasted the truth of wine
but that pleasure is hard to explain to the sober.

月下獨酌四首之二

花間一壺酒，獨酌無相親。
舉杯邀明月，對影成三人。
月既不解飲，影徒隨我身。
暫伴月將影，行樂須及春。
我歌月徘徊，我舞影零亂。
醒時同交歡，醉後各分散。
永結無情遊，相期邈雲漢。

天若不愛酒，酒星不在天。
地若不愛酒，地應無酒泉。
天地既愛酒，愛酒不愧天。
已聞清比聖，復道濁如賢。
賢聖既已飲，何必求神仙。
三杯通大道，一斗合自然。
但得酒中趣，勿為醒者傳。

MY CHINA IN TANG POETRY

The Chinese see a white rabbit pounding herbs in the moon. They also see a lady in the moon. Her name is Chang'e. Her name is tricky to pronounce, the "e" is a separate word and sounds like something between an "eh" and an "uh." Briefly, she is supposed to have stolen her husband's elixir and fled to the moon and is now up there all by herself with that pesky rabbit. More of her story is told in Volume III.

PLYING THE MOON WITH WINE

You behind the dark blue sky, when are you coming out?
I have a few questions tonight that need answering now:
I know you don't do my bidding or come just because I ask,
but if I should walk away, I'm sure you'll be right behind.
Like a flying mirror you hide behind Heaven's Coral Gates,
biding your time till the evening mists gradually fade away.
I know you come from out of the ocean in the evening,
but where do you go when dawn clouds take your place?
And does that white rabbit ever stop pounding herbs?
Is Chang'e pining away with no one to keep her company?
Are we looking at the same moon the ancients saw?
Are we no different to you than those who came before?
All I know is that us moon-gazers will all go
the way the water flows, you are the one who stays.
So, while the bottle is full and songs are keen,
why hoard your moonbeams and hide away?

SUPERSTARS

把酒問月

青天有月來幾時？我今停杯一問之。
人攀明月不可得，月行卻與人相隨。
皎如飛鏡臨丹闕，綠煙滅盡清輝發。
但見宵從海上來，寧知曉向雲間沒？
白兔搗藥秋復春，嫦娥孤棲與誰鄰？
今人不見古時月，今月曾經照古人。
古人今人若流水，共看明月皆如此。
唯願當歌對酒時，月光長照金樽裏。

"Drink Up, My Friends, Drink Up," is one he wrote when he was staying with his friend Yuan Danqui, a hermit who lived in the mountains and may have been the one who recommended him to the emperor. Prince of Chen at the end of the poem is Chen Si Wang, or Cao Zhi, a poet of the Three Kingdom's period and third son of Cao Cao.

DRINK UP, MY FRIENDS, DRINK UP

Do you not see the Yellow River
   come out of the sky
      rush down to the sea, never to return?
Do you not see noblemen mourn
   at their mirror to find hair bright
      as blue silk in the morning turn to frost at night?
Let's make the most of the good times then while they last.
There's nothing worse than an empty bottle on a moonlit night.
Heaven has given me talents, my time will surely arrive.
Money is made for spending, let it go, it will come again.

MY CHINA IN TANG POETRY

Cook the lamb, carve the ox,
here's to the three hundred cups we'll drink tonight.
Master Chen, Good Danqiu,
Drink up, my friends, drink up!
I'll sing you a song,
if you'll listen along.
I don't care for bells and drums or fine cuisine,
just let me be drunk forever, let me be.
The sages are gone and long forgotten,
only drinkers have left their names.
How is the Prince of Chen remembered
if not by the wine he served his friends?
Just because your host doesn't have much money
doesn't mean you have to drink cheap wine!
Dappled steed, sable coat,
take these to the market, my boy, and buy the best wine
    you can find.
Together we'll wash away whatever sorrow you've ever
    known!

SUPERSTARS

將進酒

君不見黃河之水天上來,
奔流到海不復回。
君不見高堂明鏡悲白髮,
朝如青絲暮成雪。
人生得意須盡歡,
莫使金樽空對月。
天生我材必有用,
千金散盡還復來。
烹羊宰牛且為樂,
會須一飲三百杯。
岑夫子,丹丘生,
將進酒,杯莫停。
與君歌一曲,
請君為我傾耳聽。
鐘鼓饌玉不足貴,
但願長醉不復醒。
古來聖賢皆寂寞,
惟有飲者留其名。
陳王昔時宴平樂,
斗酒十千恣歡謔。
主人何為言少錢,
徑須沽取對君酌。
五花馬、千金裘,
呼兒將出換美酒,
與爾同銷萬古愁。

Instead of thinking of him drowning in a drunken stupor, trying to catch the moon, I prefer to let him have his way and sail away after drinking with friends as we see in the last of these drinking poems. Note: The translation here is not line for line, I have collapsed two into one and split one into two, depending on how the rhythm of the English carries me, but it's all there!

In the middle of the poem he brings up some poets he admired: The "proud poets of the Jian An spine" refer to the Poetry of the late Han and Wei periods at the beginning of the Three Kingdoms era. Xie Tiao is called the "Younger Xie" as there is an "Elder Xie" who is Xie Lingyun, the Father of Mountain and Stream Poetry. Both Xie's were Li Bai's heroes.

AT THE TOWER BUILT BY XIE TIAO AT XUANZHOU, ON THE OCCASION OF SECRETARY SHU YUN'S FAREWELL BANQUET

Left me gone yesterday is gone nothing can stop its going.
Another tangle another day today more confusing than the
    day before.
Off they go, the autumn geese,
miles of wind ahead of them.
From this tower I drink to you,
to the immortal writings the sages left,
to the proud poets of Jian An spine,
to the clear songs Xie Tiao sung:
noble spirits flying free
up to the clear blue heights
to catch the brilliant moon.
I draw my sword to cut the water, water still flows.
I lift my cup to quench this sorrow, sorrow still grows.
If this world has no use for me,
I'll get my own raft tomorrow,
I'll let my hair down and go!

SUPERSTARS

宣州謝朓樓餞別校書叔雲

棄我去者，昨日之日不可留；
亂我心者，今日之日多煩憂。
長風萬里送秋雁，
對此可以酣高樓。
蓬萊文章建安骨，
中間小謝又清發。
俱懷逸興壯思飛，
欲上青天覽明月。
抽刀斷水水更流，
舉杯消愁愁更愁。
人生在世不稱意，
明朝散發弄扁舟。

5

From Palace to Wilderness (Part II)

Li Bai thought he'd pay his old friend a visit after he left the capital, but found, to his dismay, that the old man had died when he arrived at Si Ming, He Zhizhang's hometown. He calls He by his courtesy name, He Guizhen, as a friend would. Master Sanyin in the second poem is a famous Daoist master, and Mirror Lake is like a retirement present from the emperor.

DRINKING TO THE MEMORY OF SUPERVISOR HE
(Two Poems)

> That crazy man from Si Ming,
> that carefree He Guizhen,
> the first time we met in Chang'an,
> he called me Banished Immortal.
> He used to love a drink or two,
> but is now dust beneath the pines.
> Exchanged his gold turtle to buy us wine:
> that old memory brings tears to my eyes.
>
> When the crazy man came home to Si Ming
> Master Sanyin went out to welcome him.
> When the Emperor said goodbye, he bestowed
> Mirror Lake on him to enjoy at his leisure.

SUPERSTARS

And now he is gone, though his house remains,
and the lotus is in full bloom on Mirror Lake.
The present is empty, the past but a dream:
tears come flooding with my feelings for him.

對酒憶賀監 (二首)

四明有狂客，風流賀季真。
長安一相見，呼我謫仙人。
昔好杯中物，今爲松下塵。
金龜換酒處，卻憶淚沾巾。

狂客歸四明，山陰道士迎。
敕賜鏡湖水，爲君台沼榮。
人亡餘故宅，空有荷花生。
念此杳如夢，淒然傷我情。

In the next two poems we see Li Bai using what Matthews in his famous Chinese-English dictionary calls "pause particles," which is sounded out as "xi" 兮 and which I have used "ai" as the English equivalent. Xi is found in ancient poems from the south, for example, by Qu Yuan in *Li Sao*. Li Bai used it in quite a few of his later poems. It is an exclamation-cum-sigh. When you read it, you should draw out the vowels, so it sounds more like ai – ai – gh! It is unusual to see it used in the very personal and intimate context like "Wind Song in the Fall," as Li Bai used it here. I find it rather effective. What do you think?

MY CHINA IN TANG POETRY

WIND SONG IN THE FALL

Fall wind clear,
fall moon bright,
leaves fall together, fall apart.
Chilly crows gather, startled, fly away.
Tell me, will we ever meet again?
How am I to fight this feeling, fight this night?
Enter my door of longing and
find out what bitterness means.
How I long for you – *ai* – forever in my thoughts,
There's no such thing – *ai* – as a brief time apart.
This noose around my heart, had I known,
I'd rather not have known you from the start.

秋風詞

秋風清，
秋月明，
落葉聚還散。
寒鴉棲復，
相思相見知何日。
此時此夜難為情。
入我相思門，
知我相思苦。
長相思兮長相憶。
短相思兮無窮極。
早知如此絆人心，
何如當初莫相識。

SUPERSTARS

The Story of the Sisters E Huang 娥皇 and Nu Ying 女英

Li Bai had always loved ancient stories and did not hesitate to allude to them in his poems. As he grew older, more of them appeared in his poems. In the next poem we find the story of the sisters Huang and Ying. Yao 堯, one of the legendary kings of the Golden Age, had two daughters and nine useless sons. Thus, Yao looked elsewhere for a worthy man to inherit his kingdom. He married the daughters, E Huang and Nu Ying to Shun 舜 when he was testing Shun's strength of character. Shun proved himself worthy in multiple ways without knowing he was a candidate for the throne. Despite having married the King's daughters and was given much property, Shun continued to live modestly and even convinced his wives to follow suit. Not only that but Shun was able to transform the nine useless princes into contributing members of society. Thus, Yao judged him to be a superior man, one of virtue, integrity, and strength. Yao offered his throne to Shun, and thus began the Chinese ideal of 禪讓, *shan rang*, "meritorious inheritance of the throne" or "giving way to virtue".

In the last year of his reign, Shun was drowned in the River Xiang while touring the kingdom. When E Huang and Nu Ying heard the news, they ran to the river to mourn their king and husband. They cried so hard their tears turned to blood. Then, they threw themselves into the river to join him in death. Afterward, the bamboos in this area have spots on them that look like blood. This is what the poet is referring to at the end of the poem.

This story is used by Li Bai to evoke the age of sage kings to shame those who were supposed to be serving the present emperor of Tang. It was written around 746, soon after a political incident where many of a certain faction in Xuanzong's court were forced to commit suicide or demoted and exiled. The incident was instigated by the evil Li Linfu, who we will meet in the next chapter. This incident had to do with his attempt to replace the Crown Prince, Li Heng, who later became Emperor Suzong. Emperor Xuanzong was told by Li Linfu that the prince and his brother-in-law were meeting to plot against Xuanzong, when in fact those two were meeting about something else altogether. In the end, even though Li Heng was able to keep his place as heir apparent, he was forced to divorce his wife, and her brother was forced to commit suicide. The poem is a lament regarding the shadowy manipulations corrupting the court. By this time, Li Bai had left Chang'an but had heard about the incident from others.

TORN AWAY

Here is where their King was torn away,
torn from the sisters Huang and Ying.
Right here, south of Dongting Lake,
on the banks of the Xiaoxiang River.
Ten thousand miles deep is the ocean,
but its depth is not as deep as their grief.
Their tears shroud the sun – ai – black clouds dark.
Gibbons cry in the mist – ai – ghosts sigh in the rain.
How can my words make amends?
I fear Heaven may misconstrue my honest intent,
and send claps of thunder – ai – cracking whips.
Yao gave his throne to Shun and Shun to Yu.
When kings lose the virtuous – ai – dragons turn to fish.
When the virtuous lose power – ai – mice become tigers.
You say: Yao was jailed, Shun died forlorn.
You say: one peak is the same as the other on Jiuyi Range.
How can Shun's burial mound ever be found?
The royal sisters weeping – ai – reaches the highest clouds,
their tears gone with the windy waves – ai – never to return.

SUPERSTARS

Far away – ai – I see Cangwu's deep forests through my tears.
Not till Cangwu Mountain crumbles and Xiang waters dry
will the sisters' tears be wiped off the bamboos in the forests.

遠別離

遠別離,
古有皇英之二女,
乃在洞庭之南,
瀟湘之浦。
海水直下萬里深,
誰人不言此離苦?
日慘慘兮雲冥冥,
猩猩啼煙兮鬼嘯雨。
我縱言之將何補?
皇穹竊恐不照余之忠誠,
雷憑憑兮欲吼怒。
堯舜當之亦禪禹。
君失臣兮龍為魚,
權歸臣兮鼠變虎。
或云:堯幽囚,舜野死。
九疑聯綿皆相似,
重瞳孤墳竟何是?
帝子泣兮綠雲間,
隨風波兮去無邊。
慟哭兮遠望,
見蒼梧之深山。
蒼梧山崩湘水絕,
竹上之淚乃可滅。

Some of Li Bai's later poems are quite wild, spontaneous, and, no surprise, free. Now that you know his story, you can see why

MY CHINA IN TANG POETRY

he has gone madder than the hatter, as in the next poem. Here's some pre-reading information for comprehension:

The old warrior he was imitating is Wang Chuzhong, who used to like to chant Cao Cao's lines about being still ambitious in his old age, while beating on his jade spittoon till it broke. Li Bai made up the tonal pattern of this chant. A spittoon, which we don't see people using any more, is like a pot, usually made of metal or clay, in this case, a very fancy one, made of jade. Turn it upside down, and it would be like a long drum.

"Phoenix summons" refers to the emperor's summons and "purple mud" is what is used to seal the message. "Flying dragons" refer to the best horses in the Imperial stables.

Dong Fangshuo is a famous scholar in Emperor Wu of Han's Imperial court who was supposed to have been very humorous. He once said that he could be a hermit among all the bustle of the palaces. I have borrowed Tao Yuanming's "thatch-hut" to mean hermitage here. Tao's line: "I built my thatch-hut in the hubbub of men, but the noise of their traffic I do not hear" can be found in the Preamble to Volume II.

"Banished Immortal" is what He Zhizheng called Li Bai, which he obviously loved, and Xishi is that great beauty who is even more beautiful drunk than sober; here, Li Bai is alluding to her famous frown. The ugly women are, of course, the courtiers who tried to imitate him.

CHANTING TO THE BEAT OF MY JADE SPITTOON

Like the old warrior who chanted to the beat of his jade spittoon,
he who was too old to fight but still raring to go,
after three cups, I draw my sword to dance with the autumn moon,

break into song, sputtering through snot and tears.
The phoenix summons arrived at my door, purple mud still wet.
The emperor himself lifted his cup to welcome me.
I strode all the way to the inner sanctums of the Imperial Palaces,
and made fun of courtiers of the highest esteem.
The emperor himself gave me gifts of coral jade whips, and often sent
flying dragons from his royal stables for my ride.
Like Dong Fangshuo I built my thatch hut in the Imperial Court,
known to the chosen few as the Banished Immortal.
Like Xishi, my frown is as attractive as my smile, and copied,
to no avail, by the ugly women who made fools of themselves.
Though beloved by the emperor, in the end, envy and gossip
got the better of me, and here I am, sent packing!

玉壺吟

烈士擊玉壺，壯心惜暮年。
三杯拂劍舞秋月，忽然高詠涕泗漣。
鳳凰初下紫泥詔，謁帝稱觴登御筵。
揄揚九重萬乘主，譴浪赤墀青瑣賢。
朝天數換飛龍馬，敕賜珊瑚白玉鞭。
世人不識東方朔，大隱金門是謫仙。
西施宜笑復宜顰，醜女效之徒累身。
君王雖愛蛾眉好，無奈宮中妒殺人！

The next poem, "Tianjin Bridge" in the Third Month of the Year," is dated either 735 or 753. The admonition at the poem's end mentions three stories. They are as follow:

MY CHINA IN TANG POETRY

Li Si 李斯

The mention of yellow dogs at the end of the poem is an allusion to Li Si, who was a commoner turned small-time official in the State of Chu near the end of the Warring States Period (475-221 BCE) when China was divided into mainly seven contending states. As the story goes, he went to the outhouse one day and saw some toilet rats having a meal, but when a dog appeared, the rats ran away in fear. Then the next day, he saw more rats, this time in a barn full of harvest grains. The rats were fat and unafraid and ate to their hearts' content. Li Si had a revelation. He figured it's not what you are but where you make a living that gives you a different life. Thus, he thought that Chu was too meager a state for him. He went away for more education and experience and eventually ended up in the Qin court. Later, he was recognized by the King of Qin for his abilities as a strategist and helped the king build up his state and conquer the other six warring states to establish the Qin Dynasty. Li was promoted by the Qin Emperor all the way up to becoming his Prime Minister. As the story goes, he saw a lavish feast prepared for one of his sons one day and felt fearful that such extravagance can only bring disaster. After the Qin Emperor died, disaster indeed befell him. Just as he himself rose to the top by manipulating others, now, his enemies saw the chance to pay him back with rumors and innuendos, and unfortunately for him, the new emperor believed them. Li Si was in the end executed together with three generations of his family. Before he died, he held his son in his arms and said, "Had I known what would happen today, I would have taken my yellow dogs out for more hunts and enjoyed myself instead [of working myself up the ladder and be the target of others' envy.]"

SUPERSTARS

Green Pearl 綠珠

Green Pearl's story is Shi Chong's story. Shi Chong was a member of the literati in the third century. He became a rich man through robbery and then was given a title and got even richer. He was also tremendously extravagant. There were many stories, but I shall limit myself to two of the most outrageous. One is that he built an elaborate toilet in his home and besides making it very comfortable for his guests to use, he also made them change clothes afterwards. If a guest refused to change, he would not be allowed to visit. The second one was worse, in that people were killed. Apparently, he loved to play host and served wine to his guests. They must drink though, or else Shi Chong would execute the beautiful maiden whose job it was to persuade his guests to drink his wine. As the story goes, one time he killed three such servers because one of his guests refused to drink.

When he met Green Pearl, a singer, he fell hopelessly in love. He sent for her with the price of three buckets full of pearls as payment and received her as his concubine. He also built a resort for her which was on a hillside and many stories high. Word travelled, and one of the princes wanted Green Pearl for his own harem. Long story short, Shi Chong refused when the prince sent for her and, Green Pearl, out of loyalty to Shi Chong, jumped off one of the tall buildings. The prince did not spare Shi Chong and had him executed.

Fan Li 范蠡

Fan Li is the third character with a story mentioned in the poem, although, in the poem, Li Bai calls him by his last chosen name of Chi Yizi 鴟夷子, which means a sort of leather wine holder or bag. Obviously, there's a story behind it. But first, who is Fan

Li? He was the general who found Xishi for the King of Yue and trained her to be the spy and enchantress who destroyed the King of Wu. When he first found her, he fell in love with her, but sacrificed himself to the cause of the nation. He trained Xishi and accompanied her to the Kingdom of Wu. As one version of the story has it, when their mission was accomplished, he finally proposed to Xishi, who was happy to sail away with him. They never returned to Yue, forsaking the glamor and riches of the post-war Yue court. This is Daoist wisdom. Leave when the job is done to avoid envy and disaster.

Indeed, according to the *Shiji*, 史記 *Records of the Grand Historian*, after Fan Li left Wu, he wrote his friend, Zhong Shu, who had also been one of the key figures in the Wu-Yue conflict, saying, "When birds no longer fly, put away your best bow; when all the rabbits are dead, hunting dogs are cooked. The King of Yue has a long neck and a beak-like mouth, this kind of person can suffer hard times with you but is not one with whom you can share wealth. You should leave now." Zhong did not heed Fan Li's warning in time, and before long, was given the gift of the sword with which to commit suicide by the King of Yue. This saying from Fan Li's letter, "When birds no longer fly, put away your best bow; when all the rabbits have died, hunting dogs are cooked," 飛鳥盡，良弓藏，狡兔死，走狗烹 has become a set expression; often only rabbits and dogs make it into the expression. A person who can 'suffer hard times with you but is not one with whom to share wealth' has also come into common usage.

Now for the very strange name Fanli gave himself when he escaped to the neighboring state of Qi 齊 and changed his identity completely to become a merchant. The name is a nickname and belonged to another loyal minister, this time of Wu, who was also given the gift of the sword, that is, asked to kill himself, by the King of Wu after he had helped him win against Yue. This is the story of Wu Zixu 伍子胥.Wu Zixu's father and brother were both killed by the old king of Yue, Goujian's father, because of treacherous rumors and misunderstandings. Wu Zixu, the youngest son, escaped to the kingdom of Wu (not the same *wu*, just the same sound), hoping one day to avenge his father and his brother. He became a very important strategist and adviser to Fuchai and helped him win against Goujian. After winning, however, Fuchai did not heed Wu Zixu's repeated advice to kill Goujian when he had the chance, and in the end, lost his kingdom to Yue. Wu Zixu died for the same reasons that his father and brother died, because of vicious rumors and innuendos against him. Fucai granted him death. Before he died, he requested that his eyes be gouged out and hung on Wu's city wall so that he could see its ruin when it came to pass. When Fucai heard about it, he was so enraged that he had Wu Zixu's body thrown into a huge leather wine storage bag, (usually much smaller so one could fold it up when not in use and take it on trips), called, you guessed it, a *chi yi zi* 鸱夷子, and had him thrown into the river. The people of Wu thereafter called Wu Zixu by the name of the leather wine bag. Thus, when Fanli chose to call himself Chi Yizi, he is identifying with both the man and his fate.

In the second half of the poem are "seventy-two pairs of mandarin ducks." They allude to the splendor in the courts of the two ancient states, Zhou and Qi in the preceding lines. These images describe the extravagance of court life.

IN THE STYLE OF THE ANCIENTS: TIANJIN BRIDGE IN THE THIRD MONTH OF THE YEAR

>Tianjin Bridge in full splendor
>in the third month of the year:

MY CHINA IN TANG POETRY

peach flowers and pear blossoms everywhere.
One morning you see them, and the next,
they're gone with the waves, one lot pushing another
down the river to the east, and so it has always been.
New visitors too come every year:
on the bridge they come and go.
At cockcrow you see the courtiers
come for court, lined up outside the palace.
As the sun sets on old Luoyang,
covering half the city in shadows,
the other half comes to life.
In colorful finery, on horses like flying dragons,
with golden bridles on their heads, rushing past
pedestrians who had better move out of the way,
people in high places are in a hurry
to get home and start the next part of the day.
Guests are waiting, feasts prepared,
platters overflowing with fantastic treasures
surge through the splendid rooms, while
Zhou dancers sway with the music, filling the air
with heavenly songs of Qi. Seventy-two pairs
of mandarin ducks waddle about among them,
making love in dark corners, so they say.
Endless nights turn into days chasing hours away.
They tell themselves this scene will last forever.
Those who stay on after their work is done
should heed the lessons in history:
remember the yellow dogs who didn't get to hunt,
and Green Pearl's beauty that led to bloody death.
I will follow Fan Li's example, call myself Chi Yizi,
let my hair down and sail away on my little raft!

SUPERSTARS

古風

天津三月時，千門桃與李。
朝為斷腸花，暮逐東流水。
前水復後水，古今相續流。
新人非舊人，年年橋上游。
雞鳴海色動，謁帝羅公侯。
月落西上陽，餘輝半城樓。
衣冠照雲日，朝下散皇州。
鞍馬如飛龍，黃金絡馬頭。
行人皆辟易，志氣橫嵩丘。
入門上高堂，列鼎錯珍饈。
香風引趙舞，清管隨齊謳。
七十紫鴛鴦，雙雙戲庭幽。
行樂爭晝夜，自言度千秋。
功成身不退，自古多愆尤。
黃犬空嘆息，綠珠成釁仇。
何如鴟夷子，散髮棹扁舟。

When Li Bai wrote the above poem he had seen the best years of the Tang dynasty go by and even lived the life of the courtier. He had also seen the extreme extravagance of Xuanzong's court and saw history repeating itself in so many ways that he could almost see the An Lu Shan Rebellion coming. It happened in 755-756. Li Bai was looped into the camp of one of Emperor Xuanzong's sons who wanted to be declared emperor when his father was running away to Shu. When Xuanzong's chosen heir, Suzong, who escaped with their father, was made emperor, he rounded up his brother's men and executed most of them on his return to Chang'an. Li Bai was among the captured and was almost executed as well. Fortunately, he was saved by his friend, Guo Ziyi, who had become a high office holder in Suzong's court. Some years previous, during Xuanzong's reign, Li Bai had saved Guo by speaking up on his behalf, and now Guo returned the favor. He petitioned on Li's behalf and managed to persuade the new emperor to spare him. Li Bai's sentence was commuted from execution to exile. The next poem was written when he heard that his old friend, Secretary Shi, was also to be exiled.

"Plum Flowers Fall", alludes to an old piece of flute music in the last line. Now, plum flowers, in reality, fall in late winter or early spring. So how can they be falling in early summer here? The flute music and the immortal flute player on Gold Crane Tower are also imaginary. In other words, all good things are in the past. The Changsha reference is to Jia Yi of the ancient state of Western Han who was demoted and exiled for speaking up against the political view of the time. Gold Crane Tower is at Lake City.

LISTENING TO THE FLUTE ON GOLD CRANE TOWER WITH SECRETARY SHI

Suddenly exiled, on your way to Changsha,
you look west to Chang'an but cannot see home.
Today, there is a flute on Gold Crane Tower:
"Plum Flowers Fall" at Lake City in early summer!

與史郎中欽聽黃鶴樓上吹笛

一為遷客去長沙，
西望長安不見家。
黃鶴樓中吹玉笛，
江城五月落梅花。

SUPERSTARS

Li Bai himself was to learn soon that he was exiled to Yelang in the south. He was heading slowly in that direction. (Did he ever travel in a straight line?) On his way, he heard that Emperor Suzong had granted a universal pardon to celebrate his own return to Chang'an. Thus, the next happy poem. I remember this poem from elementary school mostly because of the gibbons. I wonder why we were taught his poem, because I don't remember them telling us the backstory. I do remember emphasis being placed on the gibbons and the beautiful scenery of White King City, which is Baidi Cheng in the Chinese.

EARLY DEPARTURE FROM WHITE KING CITY

> We waved goodbye at early dawn to White King's many-colored clouds,
> and, at day's end, we already arrived at Jiangling, a thousand miles away.
> Nonstop, gibbons on both shores, call and call, and before we knew it,
> our skiff had glided past ten thousand mountain ranges without a pause.

早發白帝城

朝辭白帝彩雲間，
千里江陵一日還。
兩岸猿聲啼不住，
輕舟已過萬重山。

At Jiangling, he ran into his uncle, who had just been demoted. They decided to take a detour together and visit Dongting Lake. Ruan Ji was one of the "Seven Sages of the Bamboo Grove" of the third century CE, much admired by Li Bai and other poets. They were hiding from the authorities, refusing to serve a corrupt government, and of course sang and wrote poems and drank a lot. Ba'ling is close by the Dongting Lake.

GETTING DRUNK WITH MY UNCLE AT DONGTING LAKE
(three poems)

> We feast in our own bamboo grove
> today, just like Ruan Ji and his nephew.
> After we have downed three full cups,
> do allow me to break into drunken ease.
>
> Singing boating songs at the top of our lungs,
> we follow the floating moon towards home.
> White gulls stay close to our helm,
> perhaps hoping to share in the feast.
>
> Just lop off the heads of these mountain peaks
> and the Xiang would flow all the way to the sky.
> Ba'ling has wine enough to keep us drunk,
> no need to fret that Dongting's fall has come.

陪侍郎叔遊洞庭醉後 (三首)

今日竹林宴，
我家賢侍郎。
三杯容小阮，
醉後發清狂。

SUPERSTARS

船上齊橈樂，
湖心泛月歸。
白鷗閒不去，
爭拂酒筵飛。

剗卻君山好，
平鋪湘水流。
巴陵無限酒，
醉殺洞庭秋。

Mi Heng 禰衡

The next poem stars Mi Heng and takes place on Parrot Island, which is in the neighborhood of Gold Crane Tower. Mi Heng was a gifted child, particularly good at debates, but proud and stubborn. Kung Rong loved him and recommended him to Cao Cao, one of the three kings of the Three Kingdoms Period. However, Cao Cao gave him to Liu Biao because he felt Mi Heng had insulted him. Liu Biao also found the young man insufferably arrogant and gave him to Huang Zu. Huang Zu's son threw a feast where he was presented with the gift of a parrot. He asked Mi Heng to write a *fu* on the spot to compete with a few others and to entertain his guests. Mi Heng wrote a poem so beautiful and fluent that the hitherto nameless island came to be called Parrot Island. Eventually, Mi Heng did manage to offend Huang as well, and Huang had him executed. Li Bai was obviously sympathetic to the talented Mi Heng, who was too proud for his own good. (Story found in the *Hou Hanshu, History of The Latter Han*.)

MY CHINA IN TANG POETRY

GAZING ON PARROT ISLAND, IN REMEMBRANCE OF NI HENG

To Cao Cao, who had his eye set on winning the world,
Ni Heng was but an ant on the ground where he trod.
Huang Ju, a small man with a narrow mind,
killed Ni Heng and became villain forever more.
Ni Heng sang in praise of the parrot in a poem,
his every stroke surpassed the competing literati,
his every word sounded off like hitting brass and jade,
his every phrase came alive, ready to fly off the page.
Birds of prey were lying in wait for this lonely phoenix,
plotting his demise. Ancient history this, yet the rage
rising in me is as if all five Great Peaks are stuck in
my heart, pressing to be released. How can I calm down
when a man of such great talent was completely overlooked,
heaven's gift thwarted by the ignorant.
And Parrot Island has since become barren,
a wasteland where no sweet grass bears to grow.

望鸚鵡洲懷禰衡

魏帝營八極，蟻觀一禰衡。
黃祖斗筲人，殺之受惡名。
吳江賦鸚鵡，落筆超羣英。
鏘鏘振金玉，句句欲飛鳴。
鷙鶚啄孤鳳，千春傷我情。
五嶽起方寸，隱然詎可平。
才高竟何施，寡識冒天刑。
至今芳洲上，蘭蕙不忍生。

SUPERSTARS

"A River Chant" is another old man poem. It sounds like something written in retrospect of the glory days when he was the emperor's favorite and invited to sail with him on the river. The ending comes from someone who had gained quite a bit of perspective since then. Qu Yuan is the poet-patriot whose king, i.e., the King of Chu, would not listen to his warning and lost his kingdom. Before Chu was lost, Qu Yuan had already drowned himself. The last line refers to the fact that Chinese rivers flow towards the south and east to the sea, and Han, like Qin, means China.

A RIVER CHANT

Punting along the river in a magnolia boat,
jade pipes and golden flutes at each end.
Fine wine enough to fill ten thousand cups,
lovely ladies to see to your every need.
Immortals are waiting for their gold crane ride,
this passenger is content to watch seagulls fly.
Qu Yuan's *Lament* takes its place with suns and moons,
but the King of Chu's palatial terraces have not survived.
If status and wealth could be bestowed forever,
the waters of Han would flow north and west!

江上吟

木蘭之枻沙棠舟，玉簫金管坐兩頭。
美酒樽中置千斛，載妓隨波任去留。
仙人有待乘黃鶴，海客無心隨白鷗。
屈平辭賦懸日月，楚王臺榭空山丘。
興酣落筆搖五嶽，詩成笑傲凌滄洲。
功名富貴若長在，漢水亦應西北流。

Some say the next poem, "On Phoenix Tower at Jinling," was written in 747 while Li Bai was wandering about after he left the capital. Some say it was written much earlier when he first visited the region, and still others place it near the end of his life, after he heard he had been pardoned. It is a seven-character *lushi*, not his favorite style, but this poem has become one of his more famous ones, and some say it has even bested Cui Hao's "Gold Crane Tower." In it he evokes two ancient periods. One is the Wu and Yue period, which we have seen a few times by now, and the other is the Jin dynasties, which was even older. The Qin and Huai are two waterways that run towards the capital, Chang'an, and as the poem tells us, they were one river divided into two at the Island of White Egrets. Thus, Sun = Emperor; floating clouds = evil or useless courtiers, and river divided = country divided. I chose Changjiang for Yangtze here because of Chang'an in the last line. In fact, Li Bai simply called it by its most ancient name, The River.

ON PHOENIX TOWER AT JINLING

On the terrace at Phoenix Tower, real phoenix used to frolic.
The terrace is empty, they have all flown on with Changjiang.
In Wu Palaces, wild vegetation has taken over tidy garden paths.
Ancient gravestones stand where Jin aristocrats used to wander.
Far away the sun half sets beyond Three Peaks under hazy skies,
The Qin and Huai are split in two by the Island of White Egrets.
The sun's brilliance is again blocked out by floating clouds.
Chang'an is once again invisible, only sadness rules the land.

SUPERSTARS

登金陵鳳凰台

鳳凰台上鳳凰遊，鳳去台空江自流。
吳宮花草埋幽徑，晉代衣冠成古丘。
三山半落青天外，二水中分白鷺洲。
總為浮雲能蔽日，長安不見使人愁。

Next comes the madman of Chu, as Li Bai calls himself in the poem. Master Kung is Confucius. As the story goes, the hermit Jie Yu tried to persuade Confucius to leave politics and go into hermitage with him by singing madly in front of his carriage a song about the corruption at court that began "O Phoenix - ai - Phoenix!" This opening has been variously interpreted as Li Bai mocking Confucius or warning Confucian scholars. Also, men of the state of Chu were freer and practiced witchcraft, whereas those of the state of Lu, Confucius' state, were about rites and rituals. Li Bai is claiming not only to be mad but immortal in this poem. He was always looking for immortals and making potions and there are some who say he might have killed himself this way; the words used here that I translated as "sage's pill" (six lines to the end of the poem) refer to a method of pill making that involved mercury and maybe even gold or gun powder that they swallowed.

"The skies of Wu" in the middle of the poem look out onto the territory that belonged to the Kingdom of Wu during the Three Kingdoms Period. "The nine veins of the Great River" refer to Yangtze's nine tributaries. Master Xie is Xie Lingyun whom we have met before. There is a line in Xie's poem where he claims to have visited Mt. Lu and looked into the smooth round boulder at the top of the mountain called "Stone Mirror". In the next line, "like stilled water", is my addition. And finally, Jade Emperor is the Daoist God, and Lu Ao is a hermit from the Warring States Period, who met a strange-looking immortal and asked him to show him around, but the immortal laughed and refused, then disappeared.

BALLAD SENT TO XUZHOU AT THE IMPERIAL COURT

I am the madman of Chu, laughing and
singing my Phoenix Song to Master Kung.
Jade green staff in my hand at dawn,
I waved goodbye to Gold Crane Tower.
I've searched the Five Great Summits for immortals,
famous peaks have ever been my beloved haunts.
Mount Lu stands side by side to the Great Dipper,
as cascading clouds spill down its mountain slopes,
its shadow cuts across the lake like a shiny black spear,
where tectonic gates, a pair of stone giants, stand guard.
An upright silver stream splashes down to three stone bridges.
Censer Peak and Double Blades gaze at each other from afar.
Among the multilayered hilltops, one rising higher than another,
emerald shades among dawn clouds color the morning light.
No birds can penetrate here at the summit only eyes can reach,
the skies of Wu where heaven meets earth in rarified space.
Up here you can see the Great River rushing on, never to return,
where ever-changing cloud shadows control earth's golden lights.
Snowy crags tumble into the nine veins of the Great River,
singing along with me, in praise of Mount Lu, our origin,
the source of my passion, at the top of this great mountain.
Stone mirror has cleansed my spirit and cleared my mind,
even though green moss covers the path left by Master Xie.
I have long ago taken the sage's pill and left this world behind,
my heart is calm like stilled water, and the Dao is clear to me.

SUPERSTARS

In the distance I see sages on rainbow clouds,
each carrying a lotus spray to the Jade Emperor.
An immortal is waiting for me beyond Heaven's Ninth Spheres,
and I'd be delighted to take Lu Ao on a tour of the Heavens.

廬山謠寄盧侍御虛舟

我本楚狂人，鳳歌笑孔丘。
手持綠玉杖，朝別黃鶴樓。
五嶽尋仙不辭遠，一生好入名山游。
廬山秀出南斗傍，屏風九疊雲錦張，
影落明湖青黛光。
金闕前開二峰長，銀河倒掛三石樑。
香爐瀑布遙相望，回崖沓嶂凌蒼蒼。
翠影紅霞映朝日，鳥飛不到吳天長。
登高壯觀天地間，大江茫茫去不還。
黃雲萬里動風色，白波九道流雪山。
好為廬山謠，興因廬山發。
閒窺石鏡清我心，謝公行處蒼苔沒。
早服還丹無世情，琴心三疊道初成。
遙見仙人彩雲里，手把芙蓉朝玉京。
先期汗漫九垓上，願接盧敖游太清。

This next poem bears the same title as a poem written in 726, on his first trip to the coast, when he was in his twenties (p.25). This one was likely written in 761 when he was sixty. It has many of Li Bai's favorite things in it. In the third to the last couplet, Stone Tiger is a fierce and cruel king in the third to early fourth century, and Gusu Terrace was the terrace the King of Wu built for Xishi.

MY CHINA IN TANG POETRY

DRINK WITH ME

Don't say no to my offer of wine, look
how the spring wind has come laughing.
Peaches and plums are like old friends
poking their flower faces in my face.
Orioles are calling from emerald trees,
the moon is sticking her nose in my wine.
Yesterday's rosy cheeks we thought would stay.
Today our hair has turned more and still more gray.
Thorns have overgrown on Stone Tiger's palace,
deer are running wild everywhere at Gusu terrace.
Ancient monuments of kings and princes
all fallen down and turned to yellow dust,
what reason can you give me for refusing my wine?
Show me anyone from history who didn't have to die!

對酒

勸君莫拒杯，春風笑人來。
桃李如舊識，傾花向我開。
流鶯啼碧樹，明月窺金罍。
昨日朱顏子，今日白髮催。
棘生石虎殿，鹿走姑蘇台。
自古帝王宅，城闕閉黃埃。
君若不飲酒，昔人安在哉。

Let us end this Li Bai selection with four little poems, all with familiar themes. The first may have been written much earlier, perhaps before his first wife died and so he might have been thinking of her. It is customary to break a branch of willow on saying goodbye; goodbyes and willows are usually by a river.

SUPERSTARS

The others are closer to the end of his life. In the last poem, Li Bai was perhaps thinking of "Spring Dawn," his old friend, Meng Haoran's famous poem in the Meng chapter in Volume II. And perhaps this poem might have been the origin of the legend of Li's drunken pursuit of the moon in the water. They are all *juejus* and all famous.

ON HEARING FLUTE SOUNDS IN THE NIGHT, SPRING AT LUOYANG

Flute music from someone's home comes on the night air,
traveling all over Luoyang with the spring wind.
You can hear willow branches breaking in the music,
no traveler is spared thoughts of home far away.

春夜洛城聞笛

誰家玉笛暗飛聲，
散入春風滿洛城。
此夜曲中聞折柳，
何人不起故園情。

MY CHINA IN TANG POETRY

SITTING ALONE ON MOUNT JINTING

Flocks of birds all flown away, all gone by.
A single cloud pointlessly comes and goes.
We face each other like two old friends,
Jinting and I, without a word, never bored.

獨坐敬亭山

眾鳥高飛盡，
孤雲獨去閒。
相看兩不厭，
只有敬亭山。

QUESTION AND ANSWER IN THE HILLS

You ask me why I hide myself among these emerald hills,
I smile but have no answer to describe the freedom I feel.
Peach flowers carried away by that mysterious traveler, the river.
I follow them to a place where no mortals have ever been.

山中問答

問余何意棲碧山，
笑而不答心自閒。
桃花流水杳然去，
別有天地非人間。

SUPERSTARS

AMUSING MYSELF

Found myself asleep holding my bottle.
Flowers falling in heaps on my clothes.
I wake to walk on the moon in the water
As birds return to the woods. Anyone there?

自遣

對酒不覺暝，
落花盈我衣。
醉起步溪月，
鳥還人亦稀。

6

The Big Picture

The pinnacle of the Tang dynasty (not quite half-way between 619-907), is reached during the reign of Tang Xuanzong (reigned 712-756), affectionately known by posterity as Tang Ming Huang, or the Brilliant Emperor of Tang. This is roughly the height of what has been called the Golden Age of Poetry in China (see "Endnote" for poetic developments). The founder of the Tang dynasty was a general by the name of Li Yuan, who called himself Emperor Gaozu. Gaozu was an efficient reformer, and the policies he established allowed his son, Taizong, to usher in the cosmopolitan era that the Tang is known to be. Taizong was the one who opened the country's doors to foreign trade and religions, and this was when Buddhism and Christianity entered freely into China to intermix with the native teachings of Daoism and Confucianism. Moreover, Taizong, albeit unintentionally, engendered the possibility for the first and only female Emperor of China. She was our Brilliant Emperor's grandmother. Her name was Wu Zetian 武則天.

Wu Zetian was born into an aristocratic family. Her father was unusually open-minded and encouraged his daughter to read and write and become well-versed in the classics. She was also able to write poetry, play musical instruments, and to speak well in public, skills traditionally reserved for men. And she was beautiful too. When she was picked to be one of Emperor

SUPERSTARS

Taizong's concubines at age fourteen, she was assigned to take care of the royal laundry, an assignment that was not unusual for a rookie concubine. One day, she found herself alone with Taizong and had the audacity to approach the emperor and start a conversation with him on history. He was not only dazzled by her beauty but amazed by her knowledge and eloquence, so much so that he made her his personal secretary. This gave her exposure to state affairs at the highest level, and she was a fast learner, and soon gained Taizong's complete trust. Her duties also brought her into contact with many young men at court and one of these was to become Gaozong, the next emperor.

When, in 649, Taizong died, Wu and all the other concubines were sent, according to custom, to a Taoist temple to shave their heads and become nuns for the rest of their lives. Then, Gaozong ascended the throne. It did not take him long to send for Wu Zetian and install her in his harem. Her presence was certainly not appreciated by Gaozong's wife, Lady Wang, and the other concubines. Worse still for them, Wu gave birth to two sons and a daughter in rapid succession. Soon after the daughter was born in 654, the infant was found dead in her crib. Some say strangled. Wu accused Lady Wang and her mother of witchcraft and persuaded Gaozong to divorce his wife and rid himself of the whole Wang clan. Some say that Wu Zetian killed the baby herself in order to frame Lady Wang and displace her.

By 660, Wu Zetian was effectively the ruler of China, although she was yet to attain a befitting title for that role. The most notable among her successes during this time were the military campaigns she organized against Korea in 668 and reduced it to a vassal state. Another significant change she made was adding poetry composition to the Imperial Exam. By this time, Gaozong had gone blind. In 674, she came up with the titles of Emperor and Empress of Heaven for themselves, and for the next nine years, Empress Wu ruled openly as monarch till Gaozong's death, upon which, she made her eldest son emperor, this was Emperor Zhongzong. He, sadly, was ineffective and had the misfortune of being caught between a fierce mother and an ambitious wife. Things did not end well for Zhongzong who was forced to abdicate to his brother, Ruizong, five years later. This son was not emperor material either and, in 690, Wu Zetian finally decided to establish her own dynasty so she could rule as supreme emperor herself. She called it the Zhou dynasty. Her rule lasted until 704 when she was finally forced to give the empire back to the Li family and the Tang dynasty was resumed. A year later, in 705, she died. She was eighty-one.

Then followed a messy period of succession struggles, until Li Longji, one of her grandsons and the future Emperor Xuanzong, restored his father Ruizong to the throne in 710. As his reward, this son was appointed heir apparent. Two years later, Ruizong abdicated in favor of this twenty-seven-year-old son. Before the dust settled though, there was another coup and enforced suicide in the family. The coup was planned by Princess Taiping, Ruizong's sister.

When it failed, Xuanzong forced his aunt to commit suicide. Xuanzong ruled from 712 to 756.

Xuanzong was, on top of being young and energetic, a bright and conscientious ruler when he first ascended the throne. More importantly, the young emperor inherited an efficient government from his father and grandmother and led the country to the zenith of the Tang Dynasty, earning the name of Brilliant Emperor from posterity. Then, he became old and tired, and wolves were at the door. Looking back dispassionately, the several years before Xuanzong set eyes on Yang Guifei may have been more fateful than 738 when he became obsessed with her. Contemplating the historical picture as a whole, one had to conclude that she was not the cause of his dissolution, but merely hastened it.

The top villain in this story, according to historians, is Li Linfu 李林甫 (Li was and still is a common Chinese last name, like Smith in English, thus, there are so many of them in our stories.) This man was to become Chief Minister to Xuanzong though he started out as a low-level staff member in Crown Prince Li Ying's court. At the time, Xuanzong's favorite concubine was Lady Wu, and therefore her sons, Li Mao and Li Qi, were closest to him as well. (This was the Li Mao to whom Yang Guifei was at first given in marriage.) Weighing the odds, Li Linfu, saw that his path to advancement was through the Wu clan as opposed to his master at the time, the Crown Prince Li Ying. Through the eunuchs, whom he had been carefully cultivating, he sent Lady Wu the message that his own preference was for Li Mao, the older of her two sons, to be Crown Prince, and that when the opportunity arose, he would work against his master, Li Ying. That was Li Linfu's first move. After that, he continued to curry favor with Lady Wu whenever he could and waited.

At the same time, he was having an affair with the wife of one of the chancellors. This woman was a distant relative of Lady Wu. Then, when in 733, this woman's husband died, Li Linfu saw his chance to make another move. Through his mistress, he managed to ask Lady Wu to recommend him to Gao Lishi, who had the emperor's ear. If Gao were to mention Li's name to Xuanzong for the position, he would stand a good chance to be promoted into the dead man's vacated seat. Nonetheless, Gao Lishi did not get to be who he was by being impulsive. Indeed, his success had as much to do with his administrative skills as with his ability to back the right horse. This eunuch was far-sighted and a very cautious man. Thus, he did not stick his neck out for Li, who was yet an unknown quantity. Instead, he sent

Lady Wu a message to let her know who the new chancellor would be, so that she could pass on that information to Li, who would then submit a petition recommending this person to the emperor. In this way, the new chancellor, Han Xiu, would end up owing Li a debt of gratitude, and when another chancellorship became available, Han was honor bound to recommend Li for it. This was how Li Linfu eventually made his way into high office.

Not only was this ambitious and cunning Li Linfu free of moral scruples, but he was also endowed with a good pair of eyes and a silver tongue. Xuanzong had grown tired of his many duties and also became increasingly superstitious and decadent. Understanding this well, Li Linfu, gradually made it easier and easier for the emperor to let him, Li Linfu, make decisions in his stead. In 736, for example, Xuanzong wanted to return to Chang'an from Luoyang when he heard that apparitions had been seen at the Luoyang palace. It was harvest season, however, and his chancellors did not favor the idea, as the Imperial train going through the villages would disrupt harvest activities. So, his ministers petitioned Xuanzong to stay longer in Luoyang. This did not please Xuanzong, but he could not come up with a reason to disagree. Li Linfu saw the emperor's dilemma and gave him a way out. He suggested the farmers could be compensated for their loss in productivity if they were allowed to pay less taxes that year. In this way, the emperor could leave immediately without worrying about their loss. This was not the best decision for the country because harvest would still be disrupted, but Xuanzong was all too happy to accept Li's suggestion.

Li was also very good at what we call net-working these days, and he was able to augment this skill with flattery and corruption. His ability to read the emperor's moods and preferences was enhanced by eunuchs and others close to the emperor from whom he could buy information. In the guise of pleasing Xuanzong by

SUPERSTARS

keeping unpleasant news from him, Li manipulated the old man and gained power and wealth for himself. By 744, Xuanzong trusted him so completely that he considered letting Li, now his Chief Minister, take over all state matters. At this point, Gao Lishi stepped in and, behind the scenes, persuaded Xuanzong not to entirely give up control. Nevertheless, from 736 until his death in 753, Li Linfu was the most powerful man in Xuanzong's court.

Now let us turn to our other superstar, Du Fu, and see how he fits into this big picture and how Li Linfu figured in his life. Du Fu was born in 712, the same year Xuanzong became Emperor. He came from a family of scholar officials. The Du family had lost their wealth over time, and even though his mother was the great-granddaughter of Emperor Taizong, she did not bring wealth into the Du family. She died soon after the birth of her eldest son, Du Fu. The boy was intelligent and conscientious, impressing his father's friends even as a child. He was brought up in the Confucian tradition and expected to become a scholar official when he grew up. At twenty-four he went to the capital for the Imperial Exam. Like many bright young men before and after him, he inexplicably failed this notoriously capricious exam. A few years later, his father died, and Du Fu became the head of the Du family. He had three half-brothers and a sister. At his father's death, he could have inherited his minor official position but allowed one of his half-brothers to do so instead. Since getting to know the country was also part of a Confucian gentleman's education, he began traveling after he settled the family in Luoyang. In 744 he met Li Bai, who was with another poet, Gao Shi, at a wine shop and ended up traveling with them. After a second accidental meeting a couple of years later, they became fast friends, although this turned out to be the last time they would ever see each other. More will be said about this Li Bai/Du Fu friendship in a later chapter.

In 747, Du Fu decided to try the Imperial Exam again. Unfortunately, he failed again. This was the infamous special exam ordered by the emperor to recruit "the best and the brightest". The exam was administered by Li Linfu who failed everyone in order to report back to the emperor the flattering news that all who were worthy were already in his service. This happened during the years when Li Linfu was becoming more and more militaristic and persuaded Xuanzong to carry out an expansionist policy at the frontier. Li was also growing more and more paranoid, and thus encouraged Xuanzong to recruit non-Han soldiers and generals for Tang's ever-growing army. This policy was driven by Li's fear of Han generals who he thought posed a greater challenge to his power. Thus, he recruited non-Han soldiers at the border whom he swore to loyalty and replaced Han generals he did not like. His immediate competition was Yang Guifei's cousin, Yang Guozong. Little did he know, it was a non-Han general who would enter the picture and bring about an uprising that almost toppled the empire. Lucky for him, he did not live to see the An Lushan Uprising.

Born in the borderlands at the frontier, An Lushan 安祿山 was called a barbarian or a Tartar. His rise in the Tang army was meteoric. In 742, he was made military governor in the Northeastern frontier. As such, he became a frequent visitor to the capital, and was a favorite of Xuanzong and his Imperial Consort. He was apparently rotund with much red facial hair and given that natural costume (to Chinese eyes at least) he often played jester at Xuanzong's court. For example, he once wrapped himself in a giant diaper and had this "baby" presented to Yang Guifei in an "adoption ceremony" he concocted in order to amuse her. Due to such wanton behavior, rumor was rampant regarding the real relationship between this adopted mother and son couple. Such stories would have disgusted the serious and respectful Du Fu.

By the time Li Linfu finally died in 753, An, the barbarian general, had risen so far up the Imperial ladder that he was able to vie with Yang Guozong for Li's position as Chief Minister. By 754, the tension between An Lushan and Yang Guozhong came to a head. Yang kept trying to turn the Emperor against An, warning him that the Tartar was headed for rebellion, while An was getting stronger and stronger at the frontier in the Northeast. Yang won Li's position, but An would outsmart him in the next round.

On learning that An was building up his army in the Northeast, Yang told the emperor that if he sent for the Tartar, An would not dare show his face because of his evil intentions. He miscalculated. When Xuanzong summoned An, the jester promptly appeared. This was early in the spring of 754. They had a good time at the Bath of Blossoms Resort, or 華清池 Hua Qing Chi Hot Springs, that Xuanzong had built for his Imperial Consort. After that gathering, Xuanzong was convinced that An Lushan was loyal to him. An then persuaded Xuanzong to appoint him General Supervisor of a large fleet of horsemen and proceeded to select thousands of fine horses from the Imperial stables. He also obtained permission to appoint hundreds of generals and colonels who were loyal only to him. Then he left the capital in the latter part of the spring of 754. As we now know, the An Lushan Rebellion happened the next year, in 755. Xuanzong realized, too late, that his Consort's "adopted son" was after his throne.

MY CHINA IN TANG POETRY

Most Chinese schoolchildren are taught the following ballad. I am sure it was one of those assigned for "dictation" in my Chinese classes mentioned in the "Prologue". In this poem, Du Fu described how the same policy that propelled An Lushan to the top, affected common men and women of the time. The poem reads almost like a newspaper or television report had he written it for today's audience.

Depending on context, cloud and sky are both possible references to the emperor because he is supposed to be the Son of Heaven. Du Fu is calling it "distant," because he is not hearing/listening to the common people. "This Warrior King" a few lines down refers to Xuanzong, and "Land of Han" and later on, "Qin" both refer to China, and Qin is especially known for its fierce fighters. What I have translated as Kokonor is Qing Hai 青海, in the north.

SOLDIERS MARCHED TO WAR, A BALLAD

War carts rumble,
horses neigh,
men running with bows and arrows at their waists.
Fathers mothers wives and children stumbling along beside them
so much confusion so much dust covered the Xianyang Bridge:
they tug at their clothes stamp their feet begging them not to go
their wailing voices rise to implore clouds in the distant sky.
I stopped one of them to ask what this is all about
and the soldier simply replied: "it's just another roundup.
Fifteen years old and they're sent north to guard the river
when they're forty they'll be sent west, ploughing the army camps.

SUPERSTARS

Some of 'em so young, village elders have to help tie up their hair,
they'll come back with a crop of white and off they'll be sent again.
They say at the frontier blood flows like sea water and still
he's not satisfied, this Warrior King of ours:
open up the land, expand, that's all we hear.
Can you believe, in this land of Han,
two hundred provinces east of the river,
in thousands of farms and villages, only brambles grow.
And say if the women get tough, say if they plough and hoe,
crops will grow just anywhere, east fields into west.
What's more, we're men of Qin, we fight till the bitter end,
our bodies driven into battlefields like dogs and chickens.
Since you ask and want to know, sir,
but we're just soldiers, who are we to complain? –
Well, take this winter for example,
our men still out west at the passes
and the district officer wants rent,
where's the rent to come from when no one's home?
What good is it having sons now,
girls are a better bet these days.
At least with a girl you can marry 'er off to a neighbor,
sons are born to be buried like rotten grass in the fields."
Have you no eyes for the Kokonor,
where long forgotten white bones litter the shore?
New ghosts unappeased and old ghosts wail,
their voices intermingle as dim rains pour.

MY CHINA IN TANG POETRY

兵車行

車轔轔,
馬蕭蕭,
行人弓箭各在腰。
耶孃妻子走相送,
塵埃不見咸陽橋。
牽衣頓足攔道哭,
哭聲直上幹雲霄。
道旁過者問行人,行人但云點行頻。
或從十五北防河,便至四十西營田。
去時里正與裹頭,歸來頭白還戍邊。
邊庭流血成海水,武皇開邊意未已。
君不聞,
漢家山東二百州,千村萬落生荊杞。
縱有健婦把鋤犁,禾生隴畝無東西。
況復秦兵耐苦戰,被驅不異犬與雞。
長者雖有問,役夫敢申恨?
且如今年冬,未休關西卒。
縣官急索租,租稅從何出?
信知生男惡,反是生女好。
生女猶得嫁比鄰,生男埋沒隨百草。
君不見,
青海頭,
古來白骨無人收。
新鬼煩冤舊鬼哭,天陰雨濕聲啾啾。

    Though he was not the only one who tried to speak for the common man, Du Fu is best known for his empathy and the "ballad" or *yuefu* is one of the forms that he perfected and used with ease whether he was speaking for the very poor or using it to describe the extremely privileged. In these poems he acted almost like a present-day reporter, except he spoke in classical poetry. The following poem depicts the Yang clan and their ostentation. According to William Hung, this poem was probably written in 753, after Li Linfu died and Yang Guozong secured his title. Again, according to Hung, by the time he died, Li had made so many enemies that he was paranoid enough to have built himself a heavily fortified mansion with reinforced walls, secret chambers and underground tunnels. He was so afraid of being murdered by those seeking revenge that none of his fifty children and numerous concubines were privy to where he slept on any given night.

"Third Day of the Third Month" is traditionally a day for picnics. The Yang sisters, "Ladies Guo and Qin," and their cousin, Yang Guozhong, Lady Guo's paramour and the "loyal Minister" at the end of the poem, were out to enjoy the nice spring day. A modern take on Du Fu's description of their clothing and hairstyles can be found in https://cfen.si/2015/01/15/wu-zetian-whips-her-hair-around-a-glimpse-at-tang-dynasty-hairstyles/ which shows some amazing hairstyles and costumes recreated for Fan Bing Bing in her portrayal Wu Zetian. Fashion remained pretty much alike for Yang Guifei.

The poem ends with the entrance onto the scene of Yang Guozhong, "the loyal minister." It is rumored that he was the eldest sister's paramour. Thus, commentators have suggested that the "catkins" falling on "duckweeds" phrase implies improprieties in sexual relationships. "Turning the seasons around" is my way of channeling Shakespeare to say something is rotten in this Imperial state to translate Du Fu's suggestion that decorum is turned upside down. The "duckweeds on the ground" is most likely a rug with patterns woven into it so the royalties could keep their feet clean.

MY CHINA IN TANG POETRY

BALLAD OF THE CHOSEN ONES

It's the Third Day of the Third Month, the air is young.
By the banks of Chang'an, the chosen ones have come:
proud and inviting, bred to entice hearts fond and true,
lithe limbs, supple joints, perfection of flesh and bones.
Embroidered skirts mirroring late spring's changing hues,
where gold and silver coax together peacocks and unicorns.
And on their heads, what do they wear?
Kingfisher feathers, jeweled leaves adorn coils and tresses.
And from behind them, what do you see?
Pearl collars, satin sashes, flowing dresses caressing curves.
Under trembling canopies, the sisters of the Pepper Rooms ride,
for the King himself has named them Ladies Guo and Qin.
On emerald plates, purple meat of camel humps piled high.
On crystal platters, arranged like scales, flesh from the sea swims by.
Rhinoceros chopsticks, bored with abundance, unhurriedly raised,
unimpressed by the mad jangle of cleavers performing fantastic feats.
Eunuchs on swift horses appear without disturbing the dust,
and while the royal chef negotiates, "The Eight Treasures of the Earth,"
sad pipes and keening drums move gods and demons to verse.
Retainers announce the late arrival of the most important guests,
as the last of these noble riders saunters up to the forbidden ground.
And even as he dismounts, quivering catkins fall like snowflakes,
melting onto duckweeds on the carpet, turning the seasons around.

SUPERSTARS

Bluebirds appear, carrying messages on his lady's red silk scarves.
Power exudes from his demeanor like heat under smoldering clay.
Tread softly, my friends, lest you catch our loyal Minister's rage.

麗人行

三月三日天氣新，長安水邊多麗人。
態濃意遠淑且真，肌理細膩骨肉勻。
繡羅衣裳照暮春，蹙金孔雀銀麒麟。
頭上何所有？翠微盍葉垂鬢唇。
背後何所見？珠壓腰衱穩稱身。
就中雲幕椒房親，賜名大國虢與秦。
紫駝之峯出翠釜，水精之盤行素鱗。
犀箸厭飫久未下，鸞刀縷切空紛綸。
黃門飛鞚不動塵，御廚絡繹送八珍。
簫鼓哀吟感鬼神，賓從雜遝實要津。
後來鞍馬何逡巡，當軒下馬入錦茵。
楊花雪落覆白蘋，青鳥飛去銜紅巾。
炙手可熱勢絕倫，慎莫近前丞相嗔！

Now that Li Linfu had died, Du Fu finally received a minor appointment. He had left his family in Fengxian when he came to Chang'an again, job hunting. Now that he had finally "got in," he was going to move them to Chang'an. The following poem was written during this time.

Right off the bat, Du Fu identifies himself as a poor working man by calling himself a "coarse cloth". As we have seen from the opening chapter on Li Bai here, people from different strata of society were allowed to wear different colors and certain kinds of fabric, and though Du Fu was a scholar he was very poor and thus had to wear coarse cloth. Of course, 布衣 *buyi* can also simply read cotton cloth. Duling was Du Fu's ancestral home. Then, he names six pairs of virtuous men who were on his mind as he embarked on this journey. They are, Ji and Qi, two legendary statesmen from the Han dynasty; Yao and Shun. two mythic emperors, and Chao and Yu, two hermit-sages who refused to serve the corrupt court of the usurpers of Han.

On his journey, he passes by Lishan 驪山, which I translated as Black Horse, because the mountain got its name from the fact that it looks like a beautiful black horse from a distance, and the character for *Li* is "beautiful horse". This is where he encounters Chiyou, who was the mythological king, the virtuous Huangdi's enemy. Du Fu is using him here to raise a fog, which is what he did in his battle against the virtuous king, The "mountain paths ... worn smooth by tread" points out that there were numerous soldiers guarding the resort against the hoi polloi. The mountain is guarded because this is where we shall find the emperor's resort, the famous Hot Springs we have heard so much about already.

At the resort, we find Yang Guifei and her sisters "Huo and Wei," and Du Fu's famous lines: "Behind Imperial Red Gates, the reek of meat and wine./ Out on the highway, shivery cold bones freeze and die."

When Du Fu leaves Black Horse, we come to two rivers: Qing and Wei. Qing is muddy, and Wei is clear; that is to say, it is difficult to tell good from evil at such times when "the official boat", the emperor and his court, that is, is irresolute ("quit its course") in the face of invasion.

SUPERSTARS

ON MY WAY FROM THE CAPITAL TO FENGXIAN INDULGING THE MIND WITH SONG IN A HUNDRED LINES

This coarse cloth from Duling
has grown old and soft in the head.
Fool, he wanted to serve his country,
shamelessly imitating the great Ji and Qi.
Coming up empty every time, of no use
to anyone, he bends his white head, but
until they nail him shut in his coffin
he will not give up, straining his eyes to covet
a living for his people. So loud his sighs,
his songs even louder, he is the butt of jokes.
Does he not delight in the open seas? Set sail
without a care for the passing of suns and moons?
Yet he has met a Prince, akin to Yao and Shun
and cannot bear to let that final curtain fall.
Does the court lack fine timbers?
On them the royal house is built,
but just as sunflowers turn to face the sun,
nature is stubborn as his heart is staunch.
See how the likes of ants and mole-crickets
dig holes in the ground for themselves,
do they envy the great whale's burden
or dream of resting in the arms of the sea?
Take life's lesson from these creatures
and stop asking the powerful for help.
Shamefaced before Chao and Yu,
yet like them he cannot break his vow.
He borrows comfort from wine and verses,
holding off the threat of sadness with his songs.

MY CHINA IN TANG POETRY

At year's end dead grass is scattered about
and cutting winds tear at the mountain's ridge.
The crossroad is dark from stars' eclipse
as this traveler starts into the core of night.
Frost so sharp it snaps open his waistband,
icy fingers so stiff they cannot tie another knot.
In the small hours he crosses Black Horse:
the Emperor's palace is perched on its highest peak.
Chiyou has brought in the frontier fogs:
mountain paths are slippery, worn smooth by tread.
Jasper hot springs heave up earth's vapors,
as feathered royal troops patrol the grounds.
Our emperor extends his hospitality till even
creepers in the woods below sway to his music.
Visitors at this resort are royal guests everyone,
no coarse cloth there, only finest silks from hands
of village wives whose husbands are whipped into giving
all they make; their labor decorates the pillars of our state.
Like baskets full at harvest, our King's thoughts
go out to his people. If his ministers were to wake
to reason, such gifts would never have gone to waste.
So many noble courtiers have flooded the court,
the virtuous must be trembling in trepidation.
And we hear that gold plates from Inner Chambers
are found in the rooms of Huo and Wei, and that
a fantastic creature holds the court in awe with perfumes
and incenses, and such things she breathes forth.
Her guests, they say, are wrapped in luscious mink,
and sad pipes play to keep their round cheeks pink.
They say guests fill their bellies with camel's foot soup,
peel sweet oranges, and nibble on juicy hothouse fruits.
Behind Imperial Red Gates, the reek of meat and wine.

SUPERSTARS

Out on the highway, shivery cold bones freeze and die.
Such is the rule that holds apart riches and rot,
the fool's mind is stunned, his words are caught.
North at the crossing where Qing meets Wei
the official boat has again quit its course.
Hordes of water pour out of the west
like headless mountains charging forth.
Did they come from the Cave of Nowhere
or did someone topple Heaven's door?
Luckily the bridge has held:
wood beams creaking underfoot
travelers help each other across
as the river thrusts wide its shores.
Old wife left in a far province, family
of ten kept apart by wind and snow.
How long can he bear to stay away?
He has finally come to share their hunger.
On entering, he hears an ominous howl,
his youngest has just starved to death.
How can he hold down his grief, when
even neighbors are mourning in the alleys.
The shame to be a father and not be able
to bring food home. So young, this one died.
Who could have thought, such an autumn crop
and the granaries out here are empty?
A scholar pays no rent and taxes,
his name is not entered for conscription.
If even his scars cannot heal, what relief
is there for the poor laborer out in the fields?
They swarm his mind, men displaced and homeless,
men marched away to fight the frontier wars.
This menace is like a flood reaching as high

MY CHINA IN TANG POETRY

as South Mountain. How halt such force?

自京赴奉先詠懷五百字

杜陵有布衣，老大意轉拙。
許身一何愚，竊比稷與契。
居然成濩落，白首甘契闊。
蓋棺事則已，此志常覬豁。
窮年憂黎元，嘆息腸內熱。
取笑同學翁，浩歌彌激烈。
非無江海志，瀟灑送日月。
生逢堯舜君，不忍便永訣。
當今廊廟具，構廈豈雲缺。
葵藿傾太陽，物性固莫奪。
顧惟螻蟻輩，但自求其穴。
胡為慕大鯨，輒擬偃溟渤。
以茲誤生理，獨恥事干謁。
兀兀遂至今，忍為塵埃沒。
終愧巢與由，未能易其節。
沉飲聊自遣，放歌破愁絕。
歲暮百草零，疾風高岡裂。
天衢陰崢嶸，客子中夜發。
霜嚴衣帶斷，指直不得結。
凌晨過驪山，御榻在嶰嵲。
蚩尤塞寒空，蹴蹋崖谷滑。
瑤池氣鬱律，羽林相摩戛。
君臣留歡娛，樂動殷樛嶱。
賜浴皆長纓，與宴非短褐。
彤庭所分帛，本自寒女出。
鞭撻其夫家，聚斂貢城闕。
聖人筐篚恩，實欲邦國活。
臣如忽至理，君豈棄此物。

SUPERSTARS

多士盈朝廷，仁者宜戰慄。
況聞內金盤，盡在衛霍室。
中堂舞神仙，煙霧散玉質。
煖客貂鼠裘，悲管逐清瑟。
勸客駝蹄羹，霜橙壓香橘。
朱門酒肉臭，路有凍死骨。
榮枯咫尺異，惆悵難再述。
北轅就涇渭，官渡又改轍。
群冰從西下，極目高崒兀。
疑是崆峒來，恐觸天柱折。
河梁幸未坼，枝撐聲窸窣。
行旅相攀援，川廣不可越。
老妻寄異縣，十口隔風雪。
誰能久不顧，庶往共饑渴。
入門聞號咷，幼子飢已卒。
吾寧舍一哀，里巷亦嗚咽。
所愧為人父，無食致夭折。
豈知秋禾登，貧窶有倉卒。
生常免租稅，名不隸征伐。
撫跡猶酸辛，平人固騷屑。
默思失業徒，因念遠戍卒。
憂端齊終南，澒洞不可掇。

    As bad luck would have it, just as he moved his family to Chang'an, the An Lushan Rebellion erupted in the winter of 755, and he had to move them again. This time he settled them in Fuzhou, far enough away so they could be out of harm's way. Being a loyal servant of his emperor, however, he felt it his duty to leave them again and follow Emperor Xuanzong and his entourage south to Shu.

7

Country Broken, Land Remains

Perhaps he missed the royal entourage's departure; for whatever reason, we find him inexplicably stuck in Chang'an for the next couple of years. The advantage of obscurity was that though he was stranded in Chang'an, An Lushan and the rebels left him alone. The following four poems were all written during this time.

A MOONLIT NIGHT

Tonight, in Fuzhou, the moon
is my wife's only companion.
Far away I think of my little ones
who have no memory of Chang'an.
Her hair white with fresh night mist,
her arms cold in the moon's embrace,
she leans at the window, wondering when
we will lean out together and let moonlight
wash the tearstains from our cheeks?

SUPERSTARS

月夜

今夜鄜州月，閨中只獨看。
遙憐小兒女，未解憶長安。
香霧雲鬟濕，清輝玉臂寒。
何時倚虛幌，雙照淚痕干。

"A Moonlit Night" and "Spring View," are *lushis*, often translated as "regulated verse." *Lushi* is a very exact form of verse-making that builds resonance between lines, and fully developed in the Tang dynasty in the hands of poets like Du Fu whose mastery can be seen in his ability to make such a poem "form-fitting" yet resonant and unforced. It is impossible to show this without a Chinese prosodic map and there is no way to fit English into the Chinese tone patterns. Focusing only on the images and the words without their tones, perhaps my reading and the two renditions of "Spring View", in addition to the one already in my Preamble, will give you some idea of how Du Fu builds this resonance. Take lines three and four or the second couplet in "Spring View", for example:

感	時	花	濺	淚，
feel	when	flowers	splatter	tears
恨	別	鳥	驚	心。
hate/sad/regret	parting	birds	startle	heart

MY CHINA IN TANG POETRY

Read conventionally, with the caesura between the first two and the last three words, we have:

Feeling for the times   + flowers splatter tears
[unhappy about the times]

Hating good-byes   + birds startle the heart

Add to that, and centering on the (seasonal) flowers and (parting) birds we get:
   Touched by the times [circumstances or the season] [falling] flowers [are like or make us] splatter tears

   People hate [leaving] and/or see birds leave [the sight of which] startles the heart

In other words, reading the second character in each line read twice (once with the first character 感時 and 恨別 and once with the third 時花 and 別鳥), in the third and fourth lines we have:
Third line: feeling for **the times** + feeling for **seasonal** flowers [or seasonal flowers in sympathy with us] splatter tears.

   And how does "flower splatter tears" but when the wind blows, and their petals fall. Or, when I see flowers bloom, "burst into color," this incongruous sight makes me splatter tears.

   Fourth line: hate to or regret **having to part** with one another **or leave** this place, my home + **parting** birds **hate to leave, startles my heart.**

   And how do "birds startle the heart" but when the flock flies away and makes a lot of noise — whoosh! or the heart is easily startled even by bird calls, because it is sad or afraid, or tired from worry, so any little noise, like bird calls are enough to startle it. Just as flowers fall in sympathy with our sad heart, our sad heart feels sympathy with the birds who have to leave and vice versa.

In the first line, Du Fu uses "mountains and rivers remain" here, but "mountains and rivers" 山河 is also how we say country, or the land which comprises of one's country, used as in "this land is your land, this land is my land." Du Fu was stuck in Chang'an, feeling anxious, as the capital was under siege. Thus, he was pulling at his hair. Men wore their hair in a bun on the top of their heads with a pin holding it in place. This is the image we are left with in the last line.

SPRING VIEW
(another two attempts)

The country in ruins, the land persists.
A city in spring lies in depths of green.
Flowers burst into color, color our tears.
Birds leave their nests, startle our hearts.
Three months now, beacons are burning.
Family letters are worth more than gold.
My white hair grown thin from plucking,
will soon be unable to hold a pin in place.

Our country is broken, the land remains.
The city locked in spring's green shades.
Tears fall with petals in a gust of wind,
lingering bird calls startle the tired heart.
Three months running, war fires burned.
What will I not give for word from home?
This crop of white, thinned from plucking,
will soon not even keep a pin in its place.

MY CHINA IN TANG POETRY

春望

國破山河在，城春草木深。
感時花濺淚，恨別鳥驚心。
烽火連三月，家書抵萬金。
白頭搔更短，渾欲不勝簪。

The "water" in the next two poems refers to Crooked Lake, 曲江, a patch of water just outside the Imperial Palace. "At Water's Edge" is a *fu,* what I have been calling "ballad", but here, I am calling it a lament. Du Fu is calling himself an old man from Shaoling because he once lived there. It is in the countryside of Luoyang not far from the capital. Also, even though he kept calling himself old, he was only in his mid-forties; people do grow old faster in those days, and during hard times. The "rainbow colors" in this poem refer to the aristocratic families. Every one of the five powerful Yang relatives and their families have their own color, and they would dress their retinue in that one color and the mistress or master of that family would ride in a carriage or a horse at the front, with Yang Guozhong at the head of the procession. Twin Blades is at Shu and is where the exiled court has run to hide. And finally, the "foreign hooves" belong to An Lushan and his army, occupying Chang'an.

AT WATER'S EDGE: A LAMENT

An old man from Shaoling stifles a sob,
hiding in spring's shadows along Crooked Lake.
The Imperial City has locked up its thousand gates,
new green rushes and willows flourish in empty display.
Yet remember when royal banners paraded down South Park,
how their rainbow colors bristled, and all things thrived?

SUPERSTARS

From the Morning Sun they came, the most exalted lady
and her king. She was his chosen, his consort, his pride.
Before the royal carriage, the best archers rode:
girls on white horses; horses chomping on bits of gold.
One arched her body, shot an arrow at the clouds:
a pair of wings appeared, fluttering to the ground.
Where are they now, dark eyes, teeth bright as the sun?
Blood-splattered wandering ghosts lost in the wilderness.
Clear waters of Wei cuts deep between Twin Blades,
those who left, left no word: those left behind, no news.
Can anyone with a heart not shed tears?
Flowers fall in the river; where do they go?
Yellow twilight shrouds the old city.
Inside, foreign hooves are raising dust.
I live south outside the city now, but my eyes
are weak and can't help but look back north.

哀江頭

少陵野老吞聲哭，春日潛行曲江曲。
江頭宮殿鎖千門，細柳新蒲為誰綠？
憶昔霓旌下南苑，苑中萬物生顏色。
昭陽殿裏第一人，同輦隨君侍君側。
輦前才人帶弓箭，白馬嚼齧黃金勒。
翻身向天仰射雲，一笑正墜雙飛翼。
明眸皓齒今何在？血污遊魂歸不得。
清渭東流劍閣深，去住彼此無消息。
人生有情淚沾臆，江水江花豈終極！
黃昏胡騎塵滿城，欲往城南望城北。

MY CHINA IN TANG POETRY

In the spring of 757, Du Fu managed to escape from Chang'an and finally made his way to Xuanzong's exiled court in Shu. By that time, he had not heard from his family for a couple of years, and since An Lushan's troops had gotten as far as Fuzhou, where he had left them, he thought it likely that they had either moved or was massacred like so many others. Thus, he was overjoyed when he finally received a letter from his wife and news that they had survived. He brought them back to Chang'an with him again, as, while he was gone, the rebels were driven out of the capital by loyal Tang forces.

Meanwhile, Xuanzong had abdicated in 756 and handed the throne over to his son, who was made Emperor Suzong. The recovery of Luoyang Palace followed in rapid succession. This was in 758. Peace did not, alas, last long. The following poem takes us back to that short-lived, semi-peaceful time in Chang'an. Here is Du Fu making the most of it and trying to be content.

AT CROOKED LAKE
(Two Poems)

Each fallen petal strips away a little bit more of spring,
wind blows its million flakes about, teasing sorrow.
Watch their last performance as these dancers say goodbye,
only wine can help ease this irksome painful feeling now.
On the lake, in summerhouses, kingfishers make nests.
In the deer park, among high tombs, unicorn-dragons rest.
From life around you deduce this rule: follow felicity.
A name is but a floating thing, why trip up the body?

From early audience every day, I take spring clothes to pawn,
head straight for the lake, get dead drunk, before going home.
Wine debts are not unusual, I have enough of those,

but a life lived to seventy, now that's a worthy boast.
Butterflies stitch elaborate designs in and out of flowers.
Dragonflies tip-toe dancing, flit, dip, and disappear.
Stories told over and over, colors and seasons recur,
do not deny each other and make the most of what's here

曲江
(二首)

一片花飛減卻春，風飄萬點正愁人。
且看欲盡花經眼，莫厭傷多酒入唇。
江上小堂巢翡翠，苑邊高冢臥麒麟。
細推物理須行樂，何用浮榮絆此身。

朝回日日典春衣，每日江頭盡醉歸。
酒債尋常行處有，人生七十古來稀。
穿花蛺蝶深深見，點水蜻蜓款款飛。
傳語風光共流轉，暫時相賞莫相違。

The reason why he had to take clothes to pawn was because suppressing the rebels had depleted the treasury and so its ministers were being paid very little and haphazardly, and Du Fu's post was a very lowly one at that.

By the autumn of 758, inevitably, "for one always eager to serve," he took his office too seriously and offended Emperor Suzong by speaking up for another official. He had been relieved of his duties when he ran into the horse in this next ballad. Through his sympathetic description of the horse and his plea for a second chance for the animal, we see Du Fu's own sentiments about being "abandoned". Mid-way in the poem, he mentions Hua Lo, a legendary horse. Two lines below that, Du Fu attributes "infectious disease" to the horse. Du Fu himself had contracted malaria, probably when he was in the south; he was in ill health for the rest of his life.

BALLAD FOR THE SKINNY HORSE

My heart hurts for that skinny horse I met on the eastern fields,
bones poking out of his shell of a body like stones out of a wall.
I tapped his hooves with his rein—he hobbled, tried to move,
almost as if he were about to gallop away as he did once before.
On looking closer, I counted six Imperial brandings in all,
everyone exclaimed he must have once belonged to the army,
abandoned here by the roadside while the troops marched on,
his skin so dry, his hair lusterless, mixed with mud and frost.
Only last year, he was among the chargers who chased away
those barbarian thieves. Like famed Hua Lo, he was chosen
for his valor and his force. A stallion from the royal stables,
he was lately laid low by infectious disease and misfortune.
Was that fatal fall inevitable for one always eager to serve?
Now he looks at us with those sorrowful eyes, as if wanting
to plead his case, eyes that used to sparkle before his master
left him under the wintry skies with wild geese for company.
Helpless against hungry birds come to feed on his open sores,
is there no shelter in a homestead nearby to take him indoors?
Give him a resting place and some sustenance, and I'm sure
he will perform for you when spring grass again grows tall.

SUPERSTARS

瘦馬行

東郊瘦馬使我傷：骨骼硉兀如堵牆。
絆之欲動轉欹側，此豈有意仍騰驤？
細看六印帶官字，眾道三軍遺路傍。
皮幹剝落雜泥滓，毛暗蕭條連雪霜。
去歲奔波逐餘寇，驊騮不慣不得將。
士卒多騎內廄馬，惆悵恐是病乘黃。
當時歷塊誤一蹶，委棄非汝能周防。
見人慘澹若哀訴，失主錯莫無晶光。
天寒遠放雁為伴，日暮不收烏啄瘡。
誰家且養願終惠，更試明年春草長。

The next horse poem is an especially intimate one for an old friend. I love the poem as it makes me think of my own dogs, one of whom is pretty old; I had brought her home from an animal shelter. We have never been to the frontier, but other than that our relationship is pretty much like that of Du Fu and his sick horse.

MY SICK HORSE

You and I have been together for a good long time,
stomping on the hilly slopes along the cold frontier.
You've done all you can to stay useful and strong,
just not strong enough to fight aging and disease.
Nothing distinguished about your pedigree,
but you have been loyal and obedient to me.
A lowly creature of little import to anyone else,
let me sing for you this sad and mournful elegy.

MY CHINA IN TANG POETRY

病馬

乘爾亦已久，天寒關塞深。
塵中老盡力，歲晚病傷心。
毛骨豈殊眾？馴良猶至今。
物微意不淺，感動一沉吟。

Next, we find another pair of fellow creatures during these hard times. Du Fu and his family were having a meal on the porch of this road-side inn and resting up to continue on their journey.

A PAIR OF SWALLOWS

A pair of swallows flew into the roadside inn, interrupting our meal.
Mud between their beaks, they are building their nest on the porch,
for they, too, are looking for shelter against the cold, wet weather,
preparing for the severe winter about to arrive.
Bringing up children in this time of dusty chaos,
like them we have come a long way from home.
This autumn finds us still alive on earth. Perhaps one day soon the time will come when we can leave these unfamiliar places.

雙燕

旅食驚雙燕，銜泥入此堂。
應同避燥濕，且復過炎涼。
養子風塵際，來時道路長。
今秋天地在，吾亦離殊方。

SUPERSTARS

Du Fu and his friend Yen Wu were both demoted and banished from court. In the next poem, Wei, the Recluse was Yen Wu. Du Fu was calling him a recluse to be polite, but Yen Wu's reclusion was not by choice. Du Fu himself was sent to various counties as a Commissioner of Education in those few years. Later on, Yen Wu, was to do quite well for himself in Chengdu and was even able to help out Du Fu and his family for a while.

This poem is of particular sentimental value to me as my mother was the one who taught it to me when I was still in elementary school and did not entirely understand what I was memorizing and reciting. Chinese children often learn poetry this way, committing poems to memory without necessarily comprehending what they were storing in their minds and then over the years as they grow up, the poems become more and more meaningful to them with maturity and life experiences. I remember particularly vividly how my mother reminded me of this poem a few years before she died, when she had just come back to North America from visiting friends in Hong Kong. She said that she didn't really enjoy going back anymore, because with each trip, the number of her old friends had dwindled, and fewer and fewer of them were left for her to visit, "just like what Du Fu said when he visited his friend Yen Wu". I reminded her of how she made me memorize this poem one summer and that I had translated it into English, to which she said, "O, so *farn gwai lo* can read Du Fu now?" (蕃鬼佬 *farn gwai lo* is Cantonese for foreign devils, mostly meant in an endearing sort of way, as used by my mother anyway).

The two stars in the first line are 參 and 商, the morning and the evening stars. I took the liberty to make them satellites to achieve the same effect without twisting the tongue by naming them in English.

MY CHINA IN TANG POETRY

FOR MY FRIEND, WEI, THE RECLUSE

Even in life people part forever,
become like satellites of different stars.
Tonight, our stars chance to come together,
and we see by the same candlelight.
Youth and health can last but so long,
both your hair and mine have gone white.
Exchanging old news, we discover,
half our friends have turned to ghosts.
Twenty long years it took me
to come and visit you again.
When I left you were not married,
now there's a group of little strangers,
crowding round to see their father's friend.
They want to know where I come from,
and before I answered all their questions,
they've set the table and brought out wine.
In the night rain they cut spring leeks,
the smell of rice and millet fill the room,
and you, my host, toast to my visit, saying,
this rare occasion calls for at least ten cups.
After ten cups we're still not drunk,
not drunk enough to forget, tomorrow
we'll be parted by the mountains,
and again, be baffled by what will come.

SUPERSTARS

贈衛八處士

人生不相見，動如參與商。
今夕復何夕，共此燈燭光。
少壯能幾時，鬢髮各已蒼。
訪舊半為鬼，驚呼熱中腸。
焉知二十載，重上君子堂。
昔別君未婚，兒女忽成行。
怡然敬父執，問我來何方。
問答乃未已，兒女羅酒漿。
夜雨剪春韭，新炊間黃粱。
主稱會面難，一舉累十觴。
十觴亦不醉，感子故意長。
明日隔山嶽，世事兩茫茫。

8

Easy Living in Hard Times

Corruption and unrest resurfaced. Finally, after all these years of separation from his family and going through the ups and downs of palace intrigue without really managing to make much difference, Du Fu decided to give in to his desire for a quiet life and writing, and hopefully to make some money as a farmer so his family wouldn't starve. He quit his position and moved his family once again out of Chang'an. For the next eleven years we find him and his family hopping from place to place, getting lucky for a while, and then having to move again for one reason or another. He was also in bad health. He had contracted malaria a while back and it kept rearing its ugly head, then he showed symptoms of rheumatism, diabetes and asthma, such ailments that affect the elderly, even though, by our standards these days he was not really that old. He was not yet fifty, even if in some poems he called himself an old man. Life was hard, however, so it was amazing how productive he was. According to those who keep count, more than three-quarters of his surviving poems were written during this time. We begin in Chengdu where the family tried to settle down, partly with the help of Yen Wu, who was now a local administrator. From the poems written at the beginning of this period, it actually sounds quite idyllic, although, it was by no means problem-free. Tibetan invasion from the west was soon to interrupt the peace, but first, four relatively happy poems.

SUPERSTARS

A VISITOR

Living here, spring water north and south of us,
great flocks of gulls come to visit every day.
Flower-strewn paths have never been swept,
my thatch door opens for the first time for you.
Dinner will be simple, the market is too far,
and I have no money to buy us pricey wine.
But there's home brew in the jug, and the guy
who lives next door is fond of a few cups too.

客至

舍南舍北皆春水，但見群鷗日日來。
花徑不曾緣客掃，蓬門今始為君開。
盤飧市遠無兼味，樽酒家貧隻舊醅。
肯與鄰翁相對飲，隔籬呼取盡餘杯。

AT THE KIOSK BY THE WATER

I bare my belly to the warm lake air,
chanting poetry softly to myself.
Water as still as my heart is calm.
Clouds drift aimlessly, desire slow.
Quiet spring slips into quiet evening,
joy fills things joyous in themselves.
East of the river, bitter war rolls on,
glancing backward furrows my brow.

MY CHINA IN TANG POETRY

江亭

坦腹江亭暖，長吟野望時。
水流心不競，雲在意俱遲。
寂寂春將晚，欣欣物自私。
江東猶苦戰，回首一顰眉。

Note: Chengdu is also called Brocade City.

SPRING NIGHT AND A WELCOME RAIN

A good rain knows its time and season,
waiting patiently for the start of spring,
following the wind, it steals into the night,
moistening all things like a quiet gardener.
Over the untrodden country paths, dark clouds loom.
Out on the calm water, a boat, a single candle glows.
Dawn shows up wet, red patches, spreading like
heavy silk brocade, popping up all over the city.

春夜喜雨

好雨知時節，當春乃發生。
隨風潛入夜，潤物細無聲。
野徑雲俱黑，江船火獨明。
曉看紅溼處，花重錦官城。

SUPERSTARS

RIVER VILLAGE

In the crook of this clear river rests our village,
summer lasts forever here, shady nooks everywhere.
In and out of our verandah, swallows come and go.
Skimming the water, seagulls stop to preen each other.
My old wife draws up a chessboard on a scrap of paper.
Our little boy hammers a needle into a fishing hook.
Just a few herbs are all this sickly old man needs.
What more can one ask for? Life is good indeed.

江村

清江一曲抱村流，長夏江村事事幽。
自去自來樑上燕，相親相近水中鷗。
老妻畫紙為棋局，稚子敲針作釣鉤。
多病所須惟藥物，微軀此外復何求。

Those few years in and out of Chengdu were probably as close as Du Fu and his family came to peaceful country life. Even so, being a scholar farmer with no income and very little property also meant much hardship. If not for distant relatives and old friends who were willing to help once in a while and those few odd jobs writing for this or that occasion, Du Fu's family would starve even more often than they already did. The hosts mentioned in "Ballad of a Hundred Worries" are these friends who might help.

MY CHINA IN TANG POETRY

BALLAD OF A HUNDRED WORRIES

Still a child at heart I was, even at fifteen,
healthy as a young bull, always on the go.
When pears and plums ripen in the eighth month in our yard,
I would climb up and down the trees a thousand times a day.
Suddenly, an old man fifty years of age has taken my place,
he sits more than he stands, sleeps more than he walks about.
Often, forcing a smile to make small talk with his hosts,
while in his mind's eye he sees a hundred worries float by.
He returns home empty-handed to the same four empty walls,
his sad wife greets him with an expression much like his own.
The kids are too young to know restraint, in hungry desperation
they yell at their father for food even as he enters the door.

百憂集行

憶年十五心尚孩，健如黃犢走復來。
庭前八月梨棗熟，一日上樹能千迴。
即今倏忽已五十，坐臥只多少行立。
強將笑語供主人，悲見生涯百憂集。
入門依舊四壁空，老妻睹我顏色同。
癡兒不知父子禮，叫怒索飯啼門東。

SUPERSTARS

AFTER AN AUTUMN STORM, THATCH ROOF BLOWN TO PIECES: A SONG

It was almost Mid-Autumn when an angry wind howled
and rolled up all three layers of thatch cover on our roof.
Clusters of dried straw blew across the river, some strewn
along its banks, some hanging onto trees, and some
whirling in the eddying puddles where water collected.
Boys from village south came to play, making fun of me:
weak and old and unable to protect my property from thieves,
they run with armfuls of my thatch into the bamboo grove.
I called after them till my voice grew hoarse and my lips bone
   dry.
What can I do but come home to lean against my cane and
   sigh?
From out of the stillness, dark clouds have gathered,
suddenly turning the autumn sunset into ink-black night.
Our cotton coverlet of many years feels cold as iron, and
my baby boy is having a bad dream, kicking and tearing it
   apart,
while at the head of the bed, water is dripping onto the still
   wet floor.
Falling and falling, no end to the tap, tap, tapping of this
   ruthless rain.
Since the Rebellion I have had little sleep. When will daybreak
and the sun come out to dry up this monstrous vapor?
If only a mansion of tens of thousands of rooms can be built
to give shelter to everyone, we should all be happy and
   unafraid
even when wind and rain should attack again.
Aye me!

MY CHINA IN TANG POETRY

If it were suddenly to rise up before my eyes, sturdy like a mountain,
I would be content, even if my hut was blown to pieces and freezing, I die!

This poem has been particularly admired for the extravagant sentiment at the end, when, during such a dire time, he thought not of himself but of those even more unfortunate. Indeed, the original says, "poor scholars," and not "one and all" in the fifth line to the end, but I can't imagine Du Fu excluding the illiterate from his imaginary "mansion of tens of thousands of rooms." This "thatch hut" is now a major cultural museum in Chengdu with statues of many other "poor scholars."

茅屋為秋風所破歌

八月秋高風怒號，卷我屋上三重茅。
茅飛渡江灑江郊，高者掛罥長林梢，
下者飄轉沉塘坳。南村群童欺我老無力，
忍能對面為盜賊。公然抱茅入竹去，
唇焦口燥呼不得，歸來倚杖自嘆息。
俄頃風定雲墨色，秋天漠漠向昏黑。
布衾多年冷似鐵，嬌兒惡臥踏裡裂。
床頭屋漏無干處，雨腳如麻未斷絕。
自經喪亂少睡眠，長夜沾濕何由徹！
安得廣廈千萬間，大庇天下寒士俱歡顏，
風雨不動安如山。
嗚呼！
何時眼前突兀見此屋，
吾廬獨破受凍死亦足！

SUPERSTARS

The next two sets of *juejus* are on very different topics. Indeed the one written "for the fun of it" is on a rather serious subject, but like an academic who has left academia, Du Fu seemed to have set himself free from restraint, not worrying about offending anyone in the literati any more.

From the first set, "Old Zhu and Mr. Yuan" in the first poem have come to mean good friends or neighbors in vernacular Chinese: 阮生朱老 or 朱老阮生. Dong Wu in the third poem is a busy destination on the Yangtze; the line simply means he can see the boats from his thatch hut, just as the faraway hills look *as if* they were perched on his window sill. Du Fu talked about how sick he was at this time and here he was showing off the many herbs and medicinal plants he had grown in his yard for himself in the fourth poem. There are many kinds of edible roots that have medicinal properties, and they grow into different shapes if they're healthy. Ginseng e.g., looks like a person.

FOUR *JUEJUS*

Bamboo so dense by the western wall I can't open our door.
Rows of pepper so thick neighbors to the north are fenced off.
Old Zhu might come for a chat and try a few ripe plums,
Brother Yuan and I can chew the fat in the tall pines' shade.

I was building a fish trap when blustery clouds chased me away,
so icy cold the sound of the fourth-month rain, I stayed
    indoors—some fierce dragons had settled in these waters
    before we came—too dangerous to retrieve my bamboo
    sticks and stack of rocks.

MY CHINA IN TANG POETRY

A pair of golden orioles call from green willow crowns.
Trains of white egrets form lines across the bright blue sky.
Half a snow-topped mountain perched nimbly on my window,
boats headed for Dong Wu wait in line outside my garden gate.

Medicinal herbs in a variety of shapes look dewy moist and ready,
shades of green overlap each other from porch to kiosk to hedge.
I won't claim to have covered the empty hills with tender shoots,
I'm happy so long as my roots grow shapely in this parched soil.

絕句四首

堂西長筍別開門,
塹北行椒卻背村。
梅熟許同朱老吃,
松高擬對阮生論。

欲作魚梁雲復湍,
因驚四月雨聲寒。
青溪先有蛟龍窟,
竹石如山不敢安。

兩個黃鸝鳴翠柳,
一行白鷺上青天。
窗含西嶺千秋雪,
門泊東吳萬裡船。

藥條藥甲潤青青,
色過棕亭入草亭。
苗滿空山慚取譽,
根居隙地怯成形。

SUPERSTARS

SIX *JUEJU*S FOR THE FUN OF IT

1.

His power grew with the weight of years, Yu Xin,[14]
that old sailor of high clouds had set free his will.
These days they scoff at that sad song he left to us,[15]
no wonder the ancients feared the unbegotten young.

2.

Wang, Yang, Lu, Luo, prescribed the style of an age;[16]
you have not stopped mocking their lack of solemnity.
When your bodies and your names are all forgotten,
they will have survived the torrents of time and change.

3.

Lu and Wang may have lost the strength of Han and Wei,
yet they possess the elegance of the *Feng* and the *Sao*.[17]
Dragon-stripes and tiger-bones served their masters well,[18]
their fine brushwork is more than any of you can attain.

4.

Who can better these masters in learning and in skill?
Who among you can claim to stand above his peers?
A fine sight, kingfishers perched on fragrant moss,
now show me a whale rider astride the deep blue sea.

---

14 Yu Xin (513-81) He served at the southern court of the Liang Dynasty during the Period of Disunion. Was sent as ambassador to Chang'an and forced to stay there for the rest of his life. His most famous work was "Ai Jiang Nan Fu" (Lament of the South); this is the song that line 3 refers to.
15 Wang, Yang, Lu and Luo are together called the "Four Masters of the Early Tang."
16 Lu and Wang as two of the four above; Han and Wei are two dynasties in which literature flourished in scope and variety.
17 *Feng* is one part of the *Book of Songs* and *Sao* is Qu Yuan's *Li Sao*. These are two of the oldest books of poetry.
18 Imperial horses, here metaphors for their styles of brushwork.

MY CHINA IN TANG POETRY

5.

Do not disdain modern men in your love for the ancient.
Direct speech and the elegant line must go hand in hand,
lest in your scramble for the tall cars of Qu and Song[19]
you find yourselves left behind, lost in Qi-Liang's dust.[20]

6.

Tell me who can overtake those who have gone before?
Stop picking on each other and build on our forefathers' work.
Let's model ourselves after the strength of the people's *Songs*,[21]
he who masters the art of learning, learns from every school.

戲為六絕句
其一

庾信文章老更成，
凌雲健筆意縱橫。
今人嗤點流傳賦，
不覺前賢畏後生。

其二

王楊盧駱當時體，
輕薄為文哂未休。
爾曹身與名俱滅，
不廢江河萬古流。

19　Qu is Qu Yuan and Song is Song Yu, his student.
20　Qi-Liang refer to the poetic styles of the Six Dynasties (280-689).
21　Songs or folk ballads in the *Book of Songs*, in short, the voice of the people.

SUPERSTARS

其三

縱使盧王操翰墨,
劣於漢魏近風騷。
龍文虎脊皆君馭,
歷塊過都見爾曹。

其四

才力應難跨數公,
凡今誰是出羣雄?
或看翡翠蘭苕上,
未掣鯨魚碧海中。

其五

不薄今人愛古人,
清詞麗句必為鄰。
竊攀屈宋宜方駕,
恐與齊梁作後塵。

其六

未及前賢更勿疑,
遞相祖述復先誰?
別裁偽體親風雅,
轉益多師是汝師!

MY CHINA IN TANG POETRY

SIX *JUEJUS*

The sun peers over the water east of my garden hedge,
clouds rise from the mud, blooming over our little hut.
Above the tallest bamboo stalks, pretty kingfishers call.
Among the shadows, baby ducks are dancing on the sand.

A profusion of pollen powdering the air,
bees and butterflies flying here and there.
Lazing in the shade, I don't want to move,
who is that visitor and what does he want?

I dug a well and wove palm leaves for its cover,
I cut into bamboo roots to make a drainage ditch.
For sailing, a small raft and a light rope will do.
Crooked alleyways crisscross our little village.

Slanting rain scratches the sole of the river-feet.
The setting sun wraps round a tree's slim waist.
A pair of yellow birds snuggling in their nest.
Out of tattered water plants, white fish leap.

Underground shoots poke through the walls.
Twisty vines climb up to pierce the ceiling.
Light and shadow weave patterns on the ground.
In the clear water, reeds entangle and twirl around.

Water moves the moon, tricks rocks to swim.
The clear stream floats clouds next to flowers.
Birds can all find their way home to roost, but
at whose home will that fisherman sleep tonight?

SUPERSTARS

絕句 六首

日出籬東水,
雲生舍北泥。
竹高鳴翡翠,
沙僻舞鶤雞。

藹藹花蕊亂,
飛飛蜂蝶多。
幽棲身懶動,
客至欲如何。

鑿井交棕葉,
開渠斷竹根。
扁舟輕裊纜,
小徑曲通村。

急雨捎溪足,
斜暉轉樹腰。
隔巢黃鳥並,
翻藻白魚跳。

舍下筍穿壁,
庭中藤刺簷。
地晴絲冉冉,
江白草纖纖。

江動月移石,
溪虛雲傍花。
鳥棲知故道,
帆過宿誰家。

MY CHINA IN TANG POETRY

The next poem was written when Du Fu and his family first came back to Chengdu after the Tibetan invasion was put down in the spring of 764. Du Fu had transplanted the four pines himself when they moved here the first time in 760.

FOUR PINES

When I first moved you here, my little trees,
you were maybe no more than three feet tall.
These three years flew by while I was away,
and now you stand next to me tall as grown men.
I pulled at your roots to make sure they are firm,
small matter if your branches are a bit battered.
You have held on to that deep shade of green,
and your trunks are straight and branches strong.
That small fence I built for you is still intact,
perhaps it helped some to keep you from harm.
How sad I would be if you had been damaged
and all your thousand needles withered and fallen.
Yet, dare I claim to be master of these woods
when so many others are still homeless and hurt?
Until now, I've been running from the bandits too,
coming home to wild grass growing everywhere.
I look around and see devastation and despair,
your happy state has been my one consolation.
A clear breeze rises to greet me,
showering my face with frosty dew.
You will see me off when old age takes me,
meanwhile, I'll wait for your branches to spread.
My life so far has been rootless, who knows
how long you and I can keep each other company.
So, when the spirit moves me, I shall sing your praise

SUPERSTARS

and let come what may, the future is always a mystery.
I will not hanker after that boast of a thousand years
to see your twists and swirls reach heaven's canopy.

四松

四松初移時，大抵三尺強。
別來忽三載，離立如人長。
會看根不拔，莫計枝凋傷。
幽色幸秀發，疏柯亦昂藏。
所插小藩籬，本亦有堤防。
終然振撥損，得愧千葉黃？
敢為故林主？黎庶猶未康！
避賊今始歸，春草滿空堂。
覽物嘆衰謝，及茲慰凄涼。
清風為我起，灑面若微霜。
足為送老資，聊待偃蓋張。
我生無根蒂，配爾亦茫茫。
有情且賦詩，事蹟可兩忘。
勿矜千載後，慘澹蟠穹蒼！

Then, in 765 his close friend and patron, Yen Wu, who had been an official in Chengdu, died. He had made it possible for Du Fu and his family to settle in the now famous thatch hut for these several years. Now, the family had to move again. This time, they settled in Kuizhou, located in the remote area of the Three Gorges: Qutang Gorge, Wu Gorge, and Xiling Gorge. They reached Kuizhou city by sailing down the Min River to the Yangtze. The city sits on a cliff overlooking a fantastic scene. This Wu Gorge is below the Wu Shan that we first visited with Li Bai in his "Suite for My Lady". Yes, this is the Witch Mountain of the cloud and rain fame. It is not only beautiful but a place that has been the site of many significant historical events. It is thus full of ghosts. The next set of two poems were written when Du Fu first arrived at Kuizhou.

TWO *JUEJUS*

1.

Lengthening daylight gives us more of spring:
the fragrance of grass and flowers in the wind,
busy swallows flitting about with mud between their beaks,
sleepy mandarin ducks luxuriating in pairs in the warm sand.

2.

Against azure waves, birds appear in specks of white.
On fresh green slopes, flowers smolder like flames.
Another year, another spring is fast passing us by,
tell me when the year will come for us to go home?

絕句二首
其一

遲日江山麗,
春風花草香。
泥融飛燕子,
沙暖睡鴛鴦。

其二

江碧鳥逾白,
山青花欲燃。
今春看又過,
何日是歸年?

SUPERSTARS

The following poem shows how Du Fu lives up to his name of being "concerned for the country, concerned for its people" 憂國憂民 as we were taught in elementary school. Again, it is another ballad prompted by people worse off than himself. It was probably written when he first arrived at Kuizhou. At the end of this poem, he asks a strange question, comparing the wood-bearers to Wang Zhaojun, the third of the "Four Great Beauties of China," just because she used to live close by? Was he saying that these women should have been beautiful too had they not been born into the harsh realities of their lives? Also, in the middle of the poem he makes a point of pointing out that these "old women" wore "twin-buns", which was how unwed women or girls wore their hair.

BALLAD OF THE WOOD-BEARERS

Their hair half-grey, the unwed women of Kuizhou,
Forty- and fifty-year-olds, all without a husband.
Our troubled times have left these virgins unwanted:
whole lives gone by, and they have nothing but bitter sighs.
The custom here is for men to sit while the women serve,
men stay indoors while women labor to bring food home.
Eight, nine out of ten women carry wood on their backs,
working all day long, from forest to market to bed.
Old women wearing twin-buns on the nape of their necks,
sometimes with flowers and leaves pinned on the side.
Risking their lives, they climb treacherous slopes, cutting firewood,
and some even go down salt mines for something else to sell.
Instead of rouge and powder, tearstains color their ruddy faces.
Winter clothes worn thin; they eke out a living on these barren rocks.

These Witch Mountain women are coarse and ugly, everyone knows,
how is it then that Zhaojun's village is but a mere stone's throw?

負薪行

夔州處女髮半華，四十五十無夫家。
更遭喪亂嫁不售，一生抱恨長諮嗟。
土風坐男使女立，應當門戶女出入。
十猶八九負薪歸，賣薪得錢應供給。
至老雙鬟只垂頸，野花山葉銀釵並。
筋力登危集市門，死生射利兼鹽井。
面妝首飾雜啼痕，地褊衣寒困石根。
若道巫山女粗醜，何得此有昭君村？

Wang Zhaojun 王昭君

As with all these legends, there are many versions to Wang Zhaojun's story. She started off as a country girl who was chosen to be courtesan in 33 BCE. Then, she was sent to the Huns as a gift to appease their King. In paintings, Wang Zhaojun is often portrayed with a pipa, a sort of lute, which was the instrument she played especially well, and riding on a horse, because of that journey she was sent on. According to the earliest version of the story, which is probably the closest to reality, she had a son by the Hunnish king, who succeeded the king after his father's death. In accordance with their tribal custom, he married her along with his father's other wives and had more sons with her. A later version of the story says that she poisoned herself rather than conform to this incestuous custom. Yet another refinement is that she had failed to find favor with the Han Emperor before she left, because she had failed to bribe the court painter Ma Yanshou, with the result that he maliciously put a blemish on her face when he painted her portrait. This last was the story I was told as a child. According to this version of the story, it was only when she had already been promised to the Hunnish king that the emperor saw her and realized with regret what a beautiful woman he was parting with. "Finally, in the thirteenth century play, *The Sorrows of Han*, she does not even consummate her marriage with the Hunnish king, but jumps into the River Amur when she crossed the Chinese border. Her grave mound, near Kui sui in Suiyuen province is said to be the only patch of green in a waste of brown." (See David Hawkes, *A Little Primer of Du Fu*, p. 175.) This is the "green grave" in Du Fu's poem. To add two more recent implausible details to Hawkes's account: in 20th Century versions of Cantonese operas that demanded "happy endings," she bore a son for the *Chinese* emperor *before* she left, and in one case returned to him after the Hun died. In another version, she committed suicide upon the Hun's death and her body was found on Chinese soil after having drifted *against* the current back to her homeland. In any case, her sacrifice for her country has been as much admired as her beauty. My mother took me to see one of these operas, but I don't remember which version of the story it was based on. I'm sure it had a happy ending because Cantonese operas always ended with a happy song.

This next poem is from a set of five called "Songs of Remembrance at Ancient Sites." It was probably written when the Du family first arrived in the area, and he went sightseeing. He uses her palace name, Ming Fei, in the poem.

MY CHINA IN TANG POETRY

SONGS OF REMEMBRANCE AT ANCIENT SITES
(Poem III of Five)

Climb the rugged mountain range and go to the Gate of Thorn.
Here, Ming Fei was born and raised, her village bears her name.
Leaving the carmine terrace she rode across the desert,
now her green grave stands alone to face the setting sun.
Painters thought they knew that face that only the spring wind knows:
when her moon-stirred ghost returns, jade-sound disturbs the night.
For a thousand years her pipa played, speaking in foreign songs,
its music carries her story, clearly telling how she was wronged.

詠懷古蹟五首
其三

羣山萬壑赴荊門，生長明妃尚有村。
一去紫台連朔漠，獨留青冢向黃昏。
畫圖省識春風面，環佩空歸夜月魂。
千載琵琶作胡語，分明怨恨曲中論。

The next set of eight poems has often been called Du Fu's Magnum Opus. It is dense but fluent at the same time, expansive and introspective. It is fanciful and realistic. I'm calling it "Autumn Songs," as in breaking into song. The Chinese title is 秋興. The character for autumn, 秋 *qiu*, incidentally, is made up of the radical for wheat and the character for fire on the right. It is one of those wonderfully expressive characters, indicating that autumn is harvest season and also a season that heralds the end of the year with its flaming colors. The second character, 興 *xing*, means to arouse or be aroused. So, the title might be translated as "Aroused, Inspired, or Brought On by Autumn," or "Autumnal Thoughts," "Autumn Awakenings," "Autumn Arousals," or, as A.C. Graham called them, "Autumn Meditations," in his popular little book, *Poems of the Late T'ang*, [Middlesex: Penguin Books, 1965]. I feel it has a little more fire in it than "meditations". Du Fu, one might say, was moved to song by the season or moved to voice his sorrow. The character for "sorrow," by the way, is 愁 *chou*, which is made up of the word for autumn on top of the heart.

AUTUMN SONGS

White dew shrivels, wounds maples deep in the woods.
Rolling along Witch Mountain chasms, dark air moans.
Waves burst riverbanks, burst into the flooded sky.
Frontier clouds swirl down to earth's swift shadows.
Chrysanthemums have opened twice: another day's tears.
A lone boat tethered to home: the old garden in the heart.
Winter clothes hurriedly measured, everywhere scissors snap.
High on White King, washing blocks pound into the night.[22]

Kuifu, lonely city, where setting suns bend shadows,[23]
where I trace the Great Dipper north back to the capital.
The gibbon's three cries indeed brought tears to my eyes.[24]
This eighth-month-raft has drifted far away from Heaven.[25]
Portraits of heroes veiled in incense denied me, my pillow
    cold.[26]

---

22 White King is an earlier name for Kuizhou City. White King is *Baidi* 白帝 in Chinese.
23 Kuifu is the same as Kuizhou city.
24 According to a fisherman's song.
25 From the legend of a fisherman who saw a raft flow out to sea and ended up in the Milky Way; here he is referring to the emperor; he is getting further rather than closer to the Imperial seat where he wants to be.
26 Referring to the ministry at Chang'an where he used to serve.

MY CHINA IN TANG POETRY

Painted parapets on this craggy mansion mute the bugle's call.
Look where the moon has fallen, a wisteria net on the rocks.
There, on the island's shore, thick rushes are caught in its mesh.

So many houses on the fortress slope, quiet in the morning light.
Again, I'm on this tower, among the kingfisher colors on the hill.
Two nights running they slept on the waves, fishing boats returning.
In autumn stillness, swallows dance, circling the crisp, clear air.
Kuang Heng, honest and outspoken, thought little of honor and fame.
Liu Xiang, great student of Confucius, yet his wish to serve denied.[27]
Young men of my school days have all done well for themselves,
in princely robes, astride high horses, they grow proud and fat.

Chang'an is a checkerboard, where the game of Siege is played.
A hundred years, after so many moves, suffering still unchecked.
Noblemen and princes come and go, a new master in every house.
Another breed is capped and robed; all's changed, changed utterly.
Up in the north mountain passes, the clamor of drums and gongs.
Dispatches sent to the western march arrive, in the end, too late.
Dragons and fishes hibernate beneath autumn's freezing riverbed.

---

27 Kuang Heng and Liu Xiang are both ministers of the Han dynasty.

SUPERSTARS

My country, where once people lived in peace, always on my mind.

Peng Lai Battlements stand face to face to South Mountain:[28]
Dewdrops gather on golden stems touching the Milky Way.
Queen Mother descends in the west, comes through Jasper Pool.[29]
Laozi's sacred purple breath fills the mountain's Folded Gates.
Clouds spread open the pheasant's tail, parting His Palace Fan[30]
and the Sun rises on dragon scales revealing His Majestic face.
And I have slept under vast waters, waking suddenly to find
I am no longer in attendance under His blue-chained arches.

Over Bird Snare Chasm, over Crooked Lake, miles and miles[31]
of wind and smoke, autumn's slate-blue chain detains the mind:
From Calyx Terrace through Narrow City, the Royal party came,
celebrating till Hibiscus Park was invaded by bitter frontier wars.
Behind pearl screens and ornamental pillars, gold cranes remain.
Above brocade hawsers and ivory masts, white gulls still circle.
Look back and take pity on that land of song and dance.

---

28 The highest level at the Imperial Palace is called Peng Lai Hall; Peng Lai Island is a mythic place where elixirs are found. Dewdrops collected in large plates placed on tall pillars are used to make elixir.
29 Queen Mother is a constellation. Also, the mythical Queen Mother of the West who bestows the recipe for immortality. In the next line, Laozi, the forefather of Daoism, is said to have ascended to Heaven on a purple cloud.
30 Palace Fan, pheasant's tail, dragon scales and blue-chained arches are all palace rituals and descriptions.
31 Bird Snare Chasm 瞿塘峽 Qutang Xia, one of the Three Gorges, is where he is in Kuizhou, Crooked Lake 曲江 and the rest of the places named are in Chang'an. I have translated Quyang Xia as Bird Snare Chasm because I wanted to preserve the vivid image that the ancient character 瞿, which describes the big eye of a bird in fright, creates.

MY CHINA IN TANG POETRY

The heart of Qin has ever been the seat of ancient kings.³²

Kun Ming Lake, monument of Han, there men learned to fight
under the banners of the Warrior King, proud in my mind's eye.³³
The Weaver works her loom, silk and shuttle in the empty night,
Stone Whale arches its back, thrashing against the autumn wind.
Zizzania seeds toss about, black clouds heavy on water,
cold dew pierces lotus pods, red seeds drop to the ground.
This frontier wasteland at sky's edge, only birds escape.
Wild waters flood the earth: one old fisherman left behind.³⁴

From Kun Wu the road twists and meanders along the Yu Su River.
Purple Peak dips its shadow into Mei Pei Lake, the Emperor's haunt:
sweet grains pecked and scattered, pickings after the parrot's feast,
phoenix perched on emerald branches, aged splendor of wutong trees.³⁵
Girls with kingfisher feathers in their hair, fill the air with spring chatter,
and we, like gods, rowed our boats, gliding gently along evening waves.

---

32   Ancient state preceding Han, Qin is the first dynasty to unite China.
33   *Han wu di*, Warrior King of Han, built a training ground for water battle here. Weaver and Stone Whale below are statues on this lake.
34   Du Fu is this old fisherman. The first six lines describe Kun Ming Lake; the last couplet takes the mind back to where he is.
35   Back in Chang'an and the past. Sometimes, the wutong tree is translated as parasol tree because of its big, green leaves. It also has a green trunk and reminds Chinese people of home.

This rainbow brush had the power then to command all Five Elements.

My white head bent low, eyes grown dim, bitter verses are all that's left.

秋興八首

玉露凋傷楓樹林，巫山巫峽氣蕭森。
江間波浪兼天湧，塞上風雲接地陰。
叢菊兩開他日淚，孤舟一系故園心。
寒衣處處催刀尺，白帝城高急暮砧。

夔府孤城落日斜，每依北斗望京華。
聽猿實下三聲淚，奉使虛隨八月槎。
畫省香爐違伏枕，山樓粉堞隱悲笳。
請看石上藤蘿月，已映洲前蘆荻花。

千家山郭靜朝暉，一日江樓坐翠微。
信宿漁人還泛泛，清秋燕子故飛飛。
匡衡抗疏功名薄，劉向傳經心事違。
同學少年多不賤，五陵衣馬自輕肥。

聞道長安似弈棋，百年世事不勝悲。
王侯第宅皆新主，文武衣冠異昔時。
直北關山金鼓振，征西車馬羽書馳。
魚龍寂寞秋江冷，故國平居有所思。

蓬萊宮闕對南山，承露金莖霄漢間。
西望瑤池降王母，東來紫氣滿函關。
雲移雉尾開宮扇，日繞龍鱗識聖顏。
一臥滄江驚歲晚，幾回青瑣點朝班。

MY CHINA IN TANG POETRY

瞿塘峽口曲江頭，萬里風煙接素秋。
花萼夾城通御氣，芙蓉小苑入邊愁。
珠簾繡柱圍黃鵠，錦纜牙檣起白鷗。
回首可憐歌舞地，秦中自古帝王州。

昆明池水漢時功，武帝旌旗在眼中。
織女機絲虛夜月，石鯨鱗甲動秋風。
波漂菰米沉雲黑，露冷蓮房墜粉紅。
關塞極天惟鳥道，江湖滿地一漁翁。

昆吾御宿自逶迤，紫閣峯陰入渼陂。
香稻啄餘鸚鵡粒，碧梧棲老鳳凰枝。
佳人拾翠春相問，仙侶同舟晚更移。
彩筆昔曾干氣象，白頭吟望苦低垂。

9

Old Friends on First Meeting

After their first accidental meeting and travel together in 744, Li Bai and Du Fu only met one more time, but the friendship forged in that year would last a lifetime. It is generally acknowledged that the younger man, Du Fu, was much more of a fan of the older poet than Li Bai was of him. This is not surprising, as Li Bai was famous by the time they met, and Du Fu was just starting out. The younger poet was not merely a wide-eyed admirer though. Much as he looked up to Li Bai's poetry and was deeply attracted to his person, he also saw the dangers Li's behavior posed. Thus, in this poem on their second meeting a few years later, he had gently warned Li Bai of his recklessness.

Ge Hong 葛洪 (283-343 CE) in the poem was a practicing Daoist who was supposed to have found the elixir of life. He firmly believed that physical immortality was possible through practicing breathing exercises and calisthenics to cultivate a healthy qi, the essence of life that courses through our bodies. He also believed that the ingesting of medicinal herbs, gold, and cinnabar was helpful to this endeavor, a belief shared by Li Bai. Ge also tried to reconcile Daoist and Confucian philosophies in the troubled times he lived in. It is no wonder then that Du Fu called on Ge Hong in this little poem to fortify his warning for his Daoist friend.

MY CHINA IN TANG POETRY

FOR LI BAI

Like thistledown we've drifted together again this fall.
Unlike Ge Hong, we have yet to find that elixir of life.
Wasting the day in drunken songs and foolish games,
for whose sake are you performing these wild antics?

贈李白

秋來相顧尚飄蓬,
未就丹砂愧葛洪。
痛飲狂歌空度日,
飛揚跋扈為誰雄?

As the Confucian Du Fu probably saw it, Li Bai had squandered his opportunities at court. If Du Fu politely included himself in the "drunken songs and foolish games," he pointedly addressed Li Bai in the last question. Chang'an, like other capital cities, was a rumor mill full of fantastic stories, and Li Bai's drunken behavior would have been commented upon and spread among the literati, and Du Fu would have heard.

Li Bai's poem for Du Fu at this apparently unexpected meeting was, characteristically, much less serious:

FOR DU FU, WRITTEN IN JEST

Found Du Fu under the noonday sun
in a big straw hat on Dumpling Hill:
so skinny you've gotten since we last met, sure hope
you're not working too hard to make verses rhyme.

SUPERSTARS

戲贈杜甫

飯顆山頭逢杜甫,
頂戴笠子日卓午。
借問別來太瘦生,
總為從前作詩苦。

As much as Du Fu worried about Li Bai's unruly behavior, he also admired his devil-may-care attitude and his flamboyant poetry. He was also able to laugh at his own meticulous tinkering, repeating a verse many times till he found it satisfactory. He must have told Li Bai about this habit of his which gave the older poet his ammunition for making fun of him. As we have seen in Li Bai's own poetry though, some of this craziness and carelessness are masks he wore for one reason or another, masks that perhaps he did not even take off for Du Fu.

Well over a decade later, Du Fu heard rumors about Li Bai's misadventure with the rebel prince. News did not travel quite so easily in those days, so here we find Du Fu's worries in his dreams in 759 even though Li Bai had been released from exile by the time Du Fu wrote the poems. Both "Dreaming of Li Bai" poems were written as *gushi* or ancient style, which is not as strict as *lushi* with regards tone pattern. Generally speaking, Li Bai preferred the freer form of the ancient style and Du Fu the stricter *lushi*, which is not surprising, given their personalities. I wonder if Du Fu used the form preferred by Li Bai here deliberately.

MY CHINA IN TANG POETRY

DREAMING OF LI BAI
(Two Poems)

Death parts us and we swallow our voices.
To live and be torn apart is endless pain.
You've been exiled to the river's south, where
malaria plagues the land. I have had no news
till you came into my dream last night.
Sick with worry and longing, I feared
it was not your living ghost: so far away
you are, and the roads are unpredictable.
Forests of maple were green when you arrived,
mountain passes pitch dark when you drifted off.
I heard the net-of-law had caught you,
how have you found wings to come?
Sinking moonbeams flooded the eaves,
as if they wanted to show me your face.
The ocean is deep, and waves toss high,
don't let those water dragons get you!

All day long, clouds drift on,
the wanderer has yet to arrive.
Three nights running I dream of you,
what have you come to tell your friend?
Goodbyes have always been hard for you,
you complain it's not easy to come so far.
Out there, wind is rough on the water
and your shaky raft threatens to sink.
At the door, hand on white head, you seem
uncertain. Has life's vision come to naught?
Yet the capital is full of swaggering hats,
you, alone, so haggard and unadorned.

SUPERSTARS

Where is that proverbial net-with-no-holes
when an aging body can find no rest?
Eternal glory in an ageless name:
cold comfort to the lonely dead.

夢李白二首

死別已吞聲，生別常惻惻。
江南瘴癘地，逐客無消息。
故人入我夢，明我長相憶。
恐非平生魂，路遠不可測。
魂來楓林青，魂返關塞黑。
君今在羅網，何以有羽翼？
落月滿屋樑，猶疑照顏色。
水深波浪闊，無使蛟龍得。

浮雲終日行，遊子久不至。
三夜頻夢君，情親見君意。
告歸常侷促，苦道來不易。
江湖多風波，舟楫恐失墜。
出門搔白首，若負平生志。
冠蓋滿京華，斯人獨憔悴。
孰云網恢恢，將老身反累。
千秋萬歲名，寂寞身後事。

The original title of the next poem is "Sending Li Twelve Bai Twenty Rhymes." There is an intimacy to the title in that Du Fu refers to the older poet's birth order: "Li Twelve Bai" is how a friend who knows you well, might address you. It is an indication that he is a close friend who knows your family and thus your birth order, although in this case Du Fu did not know his friend's family. Then, there is the technicality of twenty rhymes in forty lines. The poem is written as a *pailu*, which means, each two lines form a unit, and one could add on as many couplets as one wishes. Thus, "twenty rhymes" equal forty lines. I had to substitute "forty lines" for the "twenty rhymes" in the English simply because I am unable to produce twenty rhymes in forty English lines. Like Italian, for a different reason, it is quite a lot easier to rhyme in Chinese than in English.

The poem was probably written after he heard Li Bai had been pardoned on his way to the swamps. Even so, it was clear to him that Li Bai's official career was over. He may also have heard that Li Bai was sick. His friend was, in fact, dying. Classical Chinese poets often wrote in shorthand, by alluding to historical figures or famous events. This is like a vocabulary to them, and depending on context, one should be able to comprehend their meaning. Among their peers, other poets and scholars that is, familiarity with theses allusions is assumed. For translators, footnotes are often the only solution, and though I have generally tried to avoid them as much as possible, I have resorted to them here. I suggest you first read the poem out loud, gather what you can, then go back for a more thorough understanding via the information in the footnotes, and then reread the poem armed with that information.

SENDING FORTY LINES TO LI TWELFTH BAI

There once was a crazy man who called
you an immortal kicked out of heaven, saying
your brush can sweep rain out of the sky,
your poetry can make ghosts and spirits cry.[36]

---

36 The crazy man is He Zhizhang whom we met in the Li Bai story. He was the Palace librarian and loved Li Bai's poems so much he copied them out and showed them to all and sundry. He was also a drinking man.

SUPERSTARS

On that morning, your wings were unfurled
and your voice was heard all over Chang'an,
where even the emperor was dazzled by your splendor.
Your work will no doubt survive generations to come.
On the Imperial yacht you regaled him with poetry,
it was you who inevitably won the silk-beast-gown.[37]
In broad daylight, the Forbidden Palace was open to you,
azure clouds gape after the dust you leave behind.[38]
Soon after you begged to leave his Imperial presence,
we came together, old friends meeting for the first time.
I admired how you held fast to your hermit's ambition,
no matter if you were in favor or if you were shunned.
We poured our hearts out to each other, behaving
like the very young, encouraged by a few cups of wine:
dancing till all hours in the Gardens of the King of Liang,[39]
singing in unison along the Si Riverbank all through spring.[40]
So much talent but where can you exercise it,
so much virtue, yet no one would put it to use.
As proud and driven as Mi Heng,[41]
a scholar as poor as Yuanxian[42]
forced by hunger to beg for rice,
hounded by lies and slander,

---

[37] "Silk-beast-gown" was the prize for being the poet who was judged as having written the best poem in the competition on board the emperor's boat. Beast refers to the mythological animals that were embroidered into the silk robe.

[38] "Azure clouds" are high officials. This is a reference to Li Bai's boast about how he was allowed to just go into the inner sanctums of the palace whenever he chose because he was so favored by the emperor.

[39] Liang Dynasty, circa 500-550 CE.

[40] The river where the King of Qin failed to recover the tripod that would have given his reign legitimacy.

[41] Mi Heng is a historical figure much admired by Li Bai. We have met him before in Li Bai's Parrot Isle poem. He lived in Han times and was extremely talented and unconventional. For example, he appeared nude when summoned to perform on the drums by his then patron Cao Cao, offended him and was sent back to Kong Rong, his previous patron who had recommended him to the great man. In the end, he was killed for misbehaving and insulting another important person.

[42] Yuanxian was a student of Confucius and reputed to have been extremely poor.

sent to the tropical heat of Five Hills,
exiled to the Perilous Peaks, haunted
for years by that bird of bad omens,[43]
weeping alone before the kind qilin.
Su Wu returned in the end to the House of Han.[44]
Would Master Huang serve under the Lord of Qin?[45]
At the Feast of Qu they forgot the sweet wine,[46]
and in his prison Master Zhou made his case.[47]
What's done has already been done to you,
no one can overturn your case now, just let it go.
Old and sick you sing by the autumn river,
sighing to your only friend, the brilliant moon.
His Imperial blessings are blocked by waves,
take your moon-raft and heed your fate.[48]

---

43 The "bird of bad omen," refers one to the story of Jia Yi (200-168 B.C.) who was another highly talented and faithful servant of the court who was slandered and sent away for some time. Jia had apparently run into a sort of owl which is a bird of bad omen according to Chinese lore and wrote a poem that so impressed his emperor who summoned him back to court.
44 Here, Li Bai is Su Wu, though he would be returning to the Tang court, a wishful wish on Du Fu's part.
45 In other words, Li Bai would not have willingly served the rebel prince.
46 This alludes to the incident of a loyal minister who felt neglected because the new ruler forgot that he was served sweet wine at the royal feasts. The previous one always remembered. In other words, Xuanzong appreciated Li Bai, but his son, Suzong, the new emperor, put him in jail.
47 Either referring to a petition Li Bai wrote in prison or should write to plead his case.
48 These last two lines read: "Don't be angry (with the emperor even though) His blessings/favors are blocked by waves, / ride the moon-raft and find a fortune-teller to tell your fate." William Hung read these last four lines as: "Now I [Du Fu] am just out of my sick bed by the bank of the river/ And am singing an old man's feeble song under the autumn moon. Were it not that the Heavenly River is now beyond my reach, I would have sailed on it to make a plea for you." My reading is somewhat different.

SUPERSTARS

寄李十二白二十韻

昔年有狂客，號爾謫仙人。
筆落驚風雨，詩成泣鬼神。
聲名從此大，汨沒一朝伸。
文彩承殊渥，流傳必絕倫。
龍舟移棹晚，獸錦奪袍新。
白日來深殿，青雲滿後塵。
乞歸優詔許，遇我宿心親。
未負幽棲志，兼全寵辱身。
劇談憐野逸，嗜酒見天真。
醉舞梁園夜，行歌泗水春。
才高心不展，道屈善無鄰。
處士禰衡俊，諸生原憲貧。
稻粱求未足，薏苡謗何頻。
五嶺炎蒸地，三危放逐臣。
幾年遭鵩鳥，獨泣向麒麟。
蘇武先還漢，黃公豈事秦。
楚筵辭醴日，梁獄上書辰。
已用當時法，誰將此義陳。
老吟秋月下，病起暮江濱。
莫怪恩波隔，乘槎與問津。

"At Sky's End: Li Bai On My Mind," is a poem written about the same time. It is a five-character *lushi*. Wild geese = message carriers. Autumn waves = bad times, corrupt people.

MY CHINA IN TANG POETRY

AT SKY'S END: LI BAI ON MY MIND

A sharp wind rises off the earth.
What noble thoughts stir your heart.
Will the wild geese ever arrive?
Autumn waves take over the land.
Living off words we're bound to go hungry,
eager mountain demons snatch up passersby.
Go seek out that other restless ghost
and cast your poems into the Mi Lo.

天末懷李白

涼風起天末，君子意如何？
鴻雁幾時到？江湖秋水多。
文章憎命達，魑魅喜人過。
應共冤魂語，投詩贈汨羅。

  The Qu Yuan reference is an ominous prediction of Li Bai's mysterious end. As legend has it, Li Bai drowned himself trying to catch the moon in a drunken stupor. Over a decade later, Du Fu himself may have also met with a watery death when his boat capsized during a storm. In Qu Yuan's case, the great poet-patriot threw himself into the Mi Lo because his emperor would not listen to his warnings and enemy forces took over the country. Qu Yuan is so beloved that we still eat lotus leaf wrapped dumplings and have dragon boat races to remember him each year on the Fifth Day of the Fifth lunar month. Originally, people only ate the leftover dumplings from the festival, as the reason for them in the first place was to feed the fish in the Mi Lo so they would leave Qu Yuan's body alone. Also, the loud drums for the dragon boat races were supposed to frighten demons and fishes away as well, and for the same reason. Also, when Du Fu wrote this poem he was still under the impression that Li Bai was exiled to Ye Lang in the south. Qu Yuan was a southern poet, which was another reason why he told his friend to communicate with the old ghost.

There is another story associated with Du Fu's death that has nothing to do with a storm. According to this popular legend, Du Fu died after over-eating at a feast on a riverboat on the Xiang River. He overate because he had just come off a ten-day fast. And there was another great poet, a good friend to Li Bai, who suffered a food-related demise. I am speaking of Meng Haoran, who died, in short, of bream, (his is the first story in Volume II). Du Fu was born too late to have met Meng, who was about as much older than Li Bai, twelve years, as Li Bai was of Du Fu, eleven years. Meng died relatively young, at age fifty-one. Li Bai and Meng Haoran were also "old friends on first meeting" 一見如故, *yi jian ru gu* and "age-forgotten friends", or friends despite age differences, 忘年之交, *wang nian zhi jiao*. The Chinese have many such four-character set phrases on any topic you can think of. The use of such set phrases in your conversations is one way to show off how much you know of the Chinese language and culture.

10

Last Poems

Here are four sad poems Du Fu wrote near the end. The last poem is dedicated to one of my teachers, the poet, Charles Tomlinson, who defended my ditching of the commas in the penultimate line there. I have since ditched quite a few commas with and without his blessing.

FATIGUE

This room is cool as the bamboo's core.
A wild moon hunts corners in the yard.
Dew grows round, spills over.
Sporadic stars trick the eye.
Fireflies carry their own lights.
Water birds call to each other.
Things in contention: getting nowhere,
this watching as the clear night dies.

倦 夜

竹涼侵臥內，野月滿庭隅。
重露成涓滴，稀星乍有無。
暗飛螢自照，水宿鳥相呼。
萬事干戈裡，空悲清夜徂。

SUPERSTARS

The Wei River and hills of Qin are in Chang'an, the capital.

MISERY

Every blade of river grass calls up a new misery, each and every day.
Through Witch Canyons, cold air blows, colder than the living knows.
Why do egrets like to stand in the whirlpool of that icy water?
For whom does that lone tree display its hundreds of flowers?
Ten years now barbarian hooves have trampled our many homes.
I've been away, a guest, a stranger, grown old in this lonely city.
The waters of Wei, the hills of Qin, will we ever see them again?
Disease has overwhelmed us all. Hungry tigers roam the land.

愁

江草日日喚愁生，巫峽泠泠非世情。
盤渦鷺浴底心性？獨樹花發自分明。
十年戎馬暗萬國，異域賓客老孤城。
渭水秦山得見否？人今罷病虎縱橫。

MY CHINA IN TANG POETRY

THOUGHTS ON A NIGHT JOURNEY

Short grass bristles on the windy bank:
a wavering mast, a lone boat at night.
Stars sweep across the wild plains:
there's a moon-flood on the river.
Can a name be made by poems alone?
The man is old, ill, and must retreat.
Blown about and helpless, what is he like?
Between earth and sky, one lone sand gull.

旅夜書懷

細草微風岸，危檣獨夜舟。
星垂平野闊，月湧大江流。
名豈文章著，官應老病休。
飄飄何所似，天地一沙鷗。

FROM A HEIGHT

Wind tight against a far sky: gibbons howl, shrieking.
Island cut out in white sand: birds fly round in circles.
Infinite woodland stripped bare in infinite silence.
Endless the Great River roars out its endless course.
Ten thousand miles of desolate autumn: I am still a guest.
Age of disease, these hundred years. On the tower, alone:
thwarted broken bitter wronged frost at my temples, I am
a stumbler lately deprived even of his cup of lousy wine.

SUPERSTARS

登高

風急天高猿嘯哀,渚清沙白鳥飛回。
無邊落木蕭蕭下,不盡長江滾滾來。
萬里悲秋常作客,百年多病獨登臺。
艱難苦恨繁霜鬢,潦倒新停濁酒杯。

Endnote: Verse Forms

The oldest book of Chinese poetry is the *Shijing*, 詩經, often translated as the *Book of Songs*, mainly folk songs collected from as early as the first millennium BCE. Confucius (551 BCE-479 BCE) is said to have been its final editor. Poetry is generally referred to as *shi*, and *jing* means collection. The vocabulary and culture of the *Shijing* is associated with the northern region of China. The dominant line of a poem in the *Shijing* is four characters.

In the south comes another important collection of early poetry called the *Chu Ci* 楚辭 (dated back to The Warring States, ca. 475-221 BCE). The *Chu Ci* is made up of several books, the most important of which is the *Li Sao* 離騷, a lament attributed to Qu Yuan 屈原 (340 BCE-278 BCE). The poems in the *Chu Ci* vary in line lengths and their imagery is associated with the State of Chu 楚. Much flora and fauna are found in poetry both north and south.

During the Han Dynasty 漢 (206 BCE-227 CE) the classic *shi* 詩 with its four-character lines was revived, and a new development of poems of five- and seven-character lines emerged. In addition, there had been a Music Bureau, or department of music in court found as early as the mythical government of Huang Di, 黄帝, who has been credited with starting a whole slew of things, including astronomy, math, writing characters, sericulture, musical laws and a Chinese version of football, the taming of wild beasts, the string instrument, guqin, and even invention of upper and lower garments and the weaving and dyeing of cloth. There is little documentary evidence though that the Music Bureau existed until the Qin 秦 (221-205 BCE) and into the Han dynasties.

Some Verse Forms Popularly Used In the Tang Dynasty (618–907)

The Tang Dynasty is often referred to as the Golden Age of Poetry in China. Poets of this period freely adopted and refined past verse forms and new forms were crystallized. The *lushi*, 律詩, was perfected early in the dynasty. It is a five- or seven-character, eight-line composition with prescribed tonal and rhyme schemes, calling for parallel structure in the middle, that is, second and third couplets. It is often translated as "regulated verse" in English. Then came the *jueju* 绝句, which was an outgrowth of the *lushi*. This is a four-line, five- or seven-character poem. That means it is half a *lushi*, and thus, is often translated as "curtailed" or "truncated" verse. The tonal patterns of the *lushi* are kept but the parallel structure is made optional, although the couplet remains foundational to the form. We think of it as a *lushi* cut short. The aesthetics of the *jueju* are similar to the Japanese haiku (which was inspired by the *jueju*) in that it invites one to contemplate and further ruminate on its meaning as it ends and is judged by its economy and suggestiveness. The *pailu* 排律 also started to emerge. This is a long form of the *lushi*, and length is not prescribed, so long as it runs in couplets. These are all called New Style Verse 近體詩 in the Tang dynasty.

Then, there is the *gushi*, 古詩, with *gu* meaning "old-style" or "ancient" and *shi* meaning "verse." It was the *yuefu* 樂府 that led the way to its development with the broader use of rhyme and fewer metrical restrictions. In the Tang dynasty, its use was revived and is differentiated from regulated verse by not following, or even deliberately violating, the rules of the *lushi*.

The *yuefu* itself was a form of poetry derived from folk-ballads. Yue fu means "music/bureau," and the poetic form is named after the governmental department of music by that name. (The character "*fu*" here is not to be confused with another word, "*fu*,"

赋 of the same sound but not the same tone, and a different word altogether, meaning "ode" or "rhapsody.") The Music Bureau in the Han dynasty collected folksongs. Confucius said that folk songs represented the voice of the people. The musical scores from these songs were used for ceremonial occasions at court as well. This collection of folk poetry from the Han dynasty serves as the basis of the *yuefu* form. These poems consisted of lines of varying lengths and broke away from the older four-character line by their use of the five-character. Tang poets imitated these *yuefu* ballads and made up their own poems accordingly. Du Fu and Bai Juyi were both promoters of this form.

Poets and Dates

In Volume I: *Superstars*
Li Bai or Li Bo (Li Po)   701 – 762
Du Fu (Tu Fu)   712 – 770

In Volume II: *Floating on Clouds*
Meng Haoran (Meng Hao-jan)   689/91 – 740
Wang Wei (Wang Wei)   699 – 761
Li Ye (Li Ye)   737? – 784
Xue Tao (Hsueh T'ao)   768 – 831
Liu Caichun (Liu Ts'ai – ts'un)   uncertain
Yu Xuanji (Yu Hs'uan-chi)   844 – 871

In Volume III: *Friends and Lovers*
Liu Zongyuan (Liu Chungyuan)   773 – 819
Liu Yuxi (Liu Yushi)   772 – 842
Bai Juyi (Po Chu-i)   772 – 846
Yuan Zhen (Yuan Chen)   779 – 831
Li He (Li Ho)   790 – 816
Du Mu (Tu Mu)   803 – 852
Li Shangyin (Li Shang-yin)   812 – 858

Acknowledgements

Many of these poems have been with me since childhood, but it was in telling my mother's story after her passing that I felt the urgency of putting together these translations for others. At the same time, my friend, Virginia Raymond, suggested that we start a writing group. Nancy Vine Durling immediately responded, and since then, the three of us, with occasional visitors, have been meeting sporadically for reading and writing sessions. Virginia, an attorney and Latin American literature professor, Nancy, a medieval French scholar and translator, and I come from entirely different backgrounds, bringing fresh perspectives to each other's work, both sympathetic and critical. This variety of input reminds me of the poetry and translation workshops at Princeton where, as an undergraduate, I began to develop an eye and an ear for writing beyond myself. I must especially acknowledge my teachers, John Peck, Edmund Keeley, and Charles Tomlinson, who took my writing seriously, more so than I could have done myself, and gave me the confidence and critical training that never left me. I must also thank all the students who participated in the translation workshops I attended throughout my years at Princeton, all coming with different languages and cultures, who shared their work with me as I with them, as we pounced on each other with youthful criticism and appreciation. Among these cohorts, Nadia Benabid has remained a staunch comrade in verse long after we both left graduate school. A big thank you is due also to the Fates who led me to Earnshaw Books and the "yes" from Mr. Graham Earnshaw, whose keen eye saw the merits of this series of Tang poems and helped me launch them into the world. And, I am in debt to to my friends, Jim Earl and Laura Gibbs, who have read many of these pages and hunted down my stray commas and miscellaneous mistakes.

To my mother, who sowed the seeds of love of classical Chinese poetry in me, and to David, my life-support and partner, I have no words that can fully express my gratitude. To Su Zhong, the first person I turn to whenever I have Chinese questions, and my high school and kindergarten classmates from Hong Kong scattered all over the world who have remained close and encouraging; to Mrs. O'Connell, the fiery speech teacher at Diocesan Girls' School who first taught me how to breathe and dance to the rhythms of English poetry, how can I thank you for the gifts you have given me?

In addition, there have been sympathetic listeners that kept me afloat, both friends and strangers, some of whom are no longer with us. I am grateful to them all. At a few junctures of my writing life when I might have given up, encouragement came my way from such writers and critics as James J.Y. Liu, who was Yvonne Sung-Sheng Chang's mentor and who led her to me for the translation of Wang Wen-Hsing's important Modernist novel, *Jia Bian (Family Catastrophe),* and Wang Wen-Hsing himself; Stephen Soong, who held up an issue of *Renditions* from going to press in order to wait for my small contribution, and who was generous enough to say that he heard the Chinese poems in my English, which, apparently, was a new experience for him; and Joseph S.M. Lau, who, sadly, passed away recently, and who also showed an interest in my translations and gave me the chance to work on some stories he collected in the *Columbia Anthology of Modern Chinese Literature.* I am grateful also to have met all my students through the years, from the one who said I was the only professor who kept him awake in class, to Robert Emerson who told me my poetry "kicks ass," and Beatrice Halbach-Singh who has become a close friend and enthusiastic listener, and all my readers wherever you are, and particularly the anonymous reader, "James," who reviewed *A River in Springtime* on "Goodreads" and called it "masterful."

Finally, to my daughter, Anne 天菲, who is the guru in my life, and my son, Zachary 甘苇, prominent in my mind as representing future generations in the Chinese Diaspora as well as poetry lovers everywhere, this is for you.

Epilogue

Growing up in Hong Kong, I did not do well in Chinese classes, and often received "big eggs", meaning zeroes, for Chinese "dictation" In this context, dictation means writing out assigned texts for memorization at home, and then writing them out in class, usually from classical Chinese poetry. In addition, such "dictations" had to be done with Chinese ink brushes, not an easy task for little hands to accomplish. Being neither studious nor particularly good at rote learning, I have no fond memories of such endeavors. On the other hand, I was fortunate to have a mother who loved the Chinese classics and would "sing" or "chant" poems and tell stories from them to me, and I absorbed by osmosis. It was not until I left the British colony for college that I discovered Chinese classical poetry for myself. Or you might say, when what I absorbed was given space to bloom.

My favorite poems were from the Tang and Song periods, and my love was discovered through English translation exercises. These exercises began at the Creative Writing workshops ran by the poet John Peck when I was an undergraduate at Princeton, and I continued taking these workshops as a graduate student under such poets as Edmund Keeley and Charles Tomlinson. I shall forever be grateful to them for what they sparked and helped nurture in me. In these workshops, I learned to borrow voices, making English poetry through listening to ghosts, the ancient Chinese poets whom my mother had sung to me all those years ago. Eventually, translation became an integral part of my work as a writer.

Translations follow originals. The music, images, and ideas

in the Chinese poems I translated were not of my own creation, did not come out of my own experience. Still, the more I wrote and translated the more I came to realize the understanding translation demands is not so different from the discoveries that grew out of my own writings. In other words, all writing is translation, from thoughts to words, and all translations, especially of poetry, are works of creative writing even though reading and understanding some other person's work and his or her culture precede the translator's creation. Translation is both greedy and generous, it wishes to appropriate as it wants to share and disseminate.

Let me now turn the coin onto its other side. The expression "lost in translation" acknowledges that not everything in one culture or language can be brought into another language or culture. Translation is, if not impossible, quixotic. I do not, however, agree with those who think that what comes across in translation only reveals that which cannot be translated, which is, after all what the phrase, "lost in translation" usually implies, that is, the failure of translation. Clearly, more is demanded of the reader of translations, just as more is demanded of the citizen of one culture to engage with those of other cultures. One must first be willing to take the leap of imagination into another world, and often, another period of time, in order to be a successful reader of translations. On the other hand, the more different the culture, the more one may be looking for differences, surprises, strangeness even. Perhaps that is why so many translations of Chinese classical poems especially have been allowed, even encouraged, to sound strange, foreign, and sometimes, weird, even nonsensical. Let me assure you that although there are Chinese poets who endeavor to "make it new" and surprise readers in their own culture with experimentation and refreshing choices, Chinese poetry is no more awkward or nonsensical than

SUPERSTARS

English poetry. In other words, I am asking you to recognize poor expressions and bad poetry for what they are, and not expect or excuse them just because they are found in translations. To do so is to disrespect the art of translation, to denigrate the challenge it poses.

Since our world has simultaneously expanded and shrunk, I shall not belabor the point about the importance of cultural exchange and exposure. The shortcut to the heart of Chinese culture is through its classics. As the popular Chinese saying goes, "to the people, food is heaven." Let me add that classical poetry is second in importance to the Chinese people only to its cuisine. Chinese people everywhere quote from classical Chinese poetry, both to express themselves and to impress others. Lines from the Tang poet Li Bai's poem, "The Road to Shu is Hard," showed up in a popular rap performance in China not so long ago. There is even a rock band named Tang Dynasty in China. Classical Chinese poetry, especially Tang poetry, is very much a part of contemporary Chinese life. Beyond prosperity and power, the Tang dynasty is judged as significant also because of its receptive and adventurous characteristics. It is, as Mark Edward Lewis calls it, *China's Cosmopolitan Empire*, (The Belknap Press of Harvard University Press, 2012).

Few will disagree that the two giants or superstars of Tang poetry are Li Bai and Du Fu (also known as Li Po and Tu Fu in previous translations). There are many translations of their works into other languages, especially into English. Why, then, do I find it necessary to translate these poets again? My first answer is that translation is a performance art, and as with any great piece of music, each performance, especially the better ones, will have its own contributions to make. The second reason is that although there are many prose translations of these poems, and some in verse as well, many of these poems are still waiting to be "rescued," to use David Young's reasoning in his *Du Fu: A Life in Poetry* (Knopf, 2008). When the Modernist poet Ezra Pound spoke of "making it [poetry] new", he meant that translating another culture's poetry can be used to refresh or transform one's own culture and poetry. Some poets have even "made [their own] poetry new" with no knowledge of the language from which they were translating. Pound himself, working from a crib, without knowing Chinese at the time, had done a better job than sinologists or Chinese translators with "The River Merchant's Wife", a poem by Li Bai, whom he called by his Japanese name, Rihaku. To give any translation a fair hearing, we must remember that translation is not a secondary art but a performance art.

Music, image, meaning, context, and culture are all important to poetry, and of all these elements, music is the hardest to convey. The task I set for myself is to do the best I can with the music I hear in the original Chinese poems, which I hear in Cantonese, and bring it over into my English translations as poetry. At the turn of the last century, the Chinese translations into English, whether in Britain or in America, tended to be too sing-songy or tried too hard to force a rhyme. After Pound and the Imagists and their efforts to "make it new", English translations from the Chinese have tended towards directness or experimentation. The better poets who translate today have managed to avoid fussiness, archaic expressions, passive descriptions and the not-so-subtle rhymes and rhythms in their work. The voice of the poet-translator, however, often takes precedence over the original poet's voice, so that poems from different Chinese poets sound alike in translations done by the same English or American poet. In such cases, the poems that result should more accurately be called "appropriations" or "conversations" rather than translations. An appropriation is the result of the poet taking a Chinese poem, mixing it with his or her own experience of a similar sentiment, tailoring it to suit her or his own feel of it, and cutting or building a new poem out of it. That seems to be acceptable these days, and some interesting pieces have come from the practice, but I cannot agree with calling this exercise translation or a faithful rendition of the original.

With that, I go back to my starting point. Translations follow originals. The creativity in this act is different though no less demanding than original compositions. Translators are obliged to be true to the original even as they make the most of their own resources. To appropriate without being faithful is to circumvent the demands of the art of translation. As I see it, my role as translator is not to give my voice to the original poet, but to borrow as I lend, that is, to reproduce in English with my ventriloquist's skill the voice I hear in the Chinese, and to place again the poem where I found it, in its historical and cultural contexts as best I can. It is my duty, in translating, to attempt to differentiate each individual poet's style one from the other. I am helped in this last challenge by the Chinese poet's own choice of form and content, as well as by his or her own personality and the stories they tell. Those interested in prosody should consult my chapter on "Verse Forms" at the end of each volume.

My China in Tang Poetry is the culmination of all the above discoveries, driven not only by my own love of the stories and poems but also by my desire to make what I know and love accessible to others who have no Chinese, at least, no classical Chinese and therefore have no way into that world. This series is my offer to take you with me to visit my ghosts.

About The Author

Susan Wan Dolling is a Chinese American writer who was born in Hong Kong, attended the Diocesan Girls' School, studied in Japan, and graduated from Princeton University with an AB in English and Creative Writing PhD in Comparative Literature. She has taught English and Literature at Fordham University and Chinese Literature at the University of Texas at Austin. Her translations of modern Chinese literature and classical Chinese poetry can be found in such publications as *Another Chicago Magazine*, *Poetry Magazine*, *Words Without Border*, *Two Lines*, *The Columbia Anthology of Modern Chinese Literature*, and *Renditions*. Her translation of Wang Wen-Hsing's Modernist novel, *Family Catastrophe* is in University of Hawaii Press's Fiction from Modern China Series. *Superstars*, *Floating on Clouds* and *Friends and Lovers*, the three volumes of stories, readings, and translations in the series, *My China in Tang Poetry*, was published in 2024 by Earnshaw Books. Most recently, she and her cello teacher, Dr. Chi-Hui Kao, has formed a musical duo called "Note After Note." For more on Susan and her work, please visit www.susanwandolling.com.

www.ingramcontent.com/pod-product-compliance
Ingram Content Group UK Ltd.
Pitfield, Milton Keynes, MK11 3LW, UK
UKHW022237230426
12048UKWH00018BA/1307